Why You Suck At Boxing

Identify and Correct Common Boxing Mistakes

Andrew Hudson

© Copyright 2025 - All rights reserved.

The content contained within this book may not be reproduced, duplicated, or transmitted without direct written permission from the author or the publisher. Under no circumstances will any blame or legal responsibility be held against the publisher, or author, for any damages, reparation, or monetary loss due to the information contained within this book, either directly or indirectly.

Legal Notice:
This book is copyright protected. It is only for personal use. You cannot amend, distribute, sell, use, quote, or paraphrase any part, or the content within this book, without the consent of the author or publisher.

Disclaimer Notice:
Please note the information contained within this document is for educational and entertainment purposes only. All effort has been executed to present accurate, up-to-date, reliable, and complete information. No warranties of any kind are declared or implied. Readers acknowledge that the author is not engaged in the rendering of legal, financial, medical, or professional advice. The content within this book has been derived from various sources. Please consult a licensed professional before attempting any techniques outlined in this book.

By reading this document, the reader agrees that under no circumstances is the author responsible for any losses, direct or indirect, that are incurred as a result of the use of the information contained within this document, including, but not limited to, errors, omissions, or inaccuracies.

Table of Contents

Introduction 5
   The Sweet Science 9
   About Me 12
   Why Boxing? 14
   This Guide 17

1. Success Is No Accident 21
   Improving Efficiently 22
   Don't Fear Your Mistakes 39

2. The Most Common Mistake 41
   The Antidote to Doubt 44
   How to Stay Mentally Strong 49

3. Your Sloppy Stance 62
   Finding Your Stance 63
   Correcting Common Mistakes 68

4. Your Clumsy Footwork 89
   The Basics of How to Step and Move 90
   Intermediate Movement and Footwork Concepts 96

5. Your Weak Punches 120
   The Basics of Punching 121
   Common Technical Errors 129
   Intermediate Attacking Concepts 141
   Common Punching Errors 152
   How to Fix Common Punching Errors 154

6. Your Poor Defense 156
    Basic Defensive Techniques 158
    Drills to Improve Your Defense 161
    Common Defensive Technical Mistakes 167
7. Common Training Mistakes 178
    Training Too Fast 179
    Breaking Line of Sight 181
    Wasting Energy 183
    Too Much Focus on the Upper Body 185
    Rule 1 and Rule 2 of Every Good Gym 186
    Tips to Make Your Training More Effective 194
8. Continuous Improvement 201
Conclusion 207
References 209

Introduction

A few months had passed since the first time I stepped into the gym. Although time flew by, I'd been feeling more and more frustrated about how I kept on making the same mistakes every single session. When I practiced my techniques in front of a mirror or with the coach watching, I was able to see some of my little technical errors and correct them by slowing down my movements and concentrating, but once I tried to speed up a bit, do more free-form practice or use these movements in sparring, it seemed like all my errors came rushing back.

The coach was patient with me and told me I'd "get it" sooner or later, but inside I was furious with myself. I could see other boxers in the gym "getting it" straight away. Why couldn't I? Was I just not cut out for boxing? Does boxing require some natural talent or ability that I just wasn't born with? All these thoughts bounced around my head, and I gradually started to question whether all these months of hard work were really worth it. I started wondering if maybe I should cut my losses and give up on my dreams of learning to box well.

Well, you know the end of the story is that I didn't give up; otherwise, I wouldn't be writing this guide. What you must be wondering is, why not? Why did I stick with it and how did I overcome this frustration and eventually improve my boxing ability enough to become a successful boxing coach in my own right? Well, that's what this whole book is about.

Let me begin with the catalyst. I had been training for about six months when it happened. I was still making the same mistakes and doubting myself more and more each day. I had done a bit of light sparring at the end of most sessions, mainly with the instructor and advanced students who knew to take it easy on me but still made my constant mistakes obvious.

A new boxer showed up at the gym, and by chance, I happened to be the only guy available to spar with him. Well, it turned out he was new to the gym, but not to boxing, and despite being a bit smaller and looking like he did not pose a threat at first glance, he made me look like an idiot. I kept tripping over my own feet as I tried to find the right distance; every punch I threw seemed like it missed by a foot or landed with zero impact, and it felt like he landed everything he threw unless I completely turtled up or practically ran away. That was the day I told myself to quit boxing, "forever".

The next session though, I went back. Rather than quit, I decided to take my fate into my own hands. Rather than waiting for myself to just "get it" as the coach had told me, I brought a new attitude into my personal development. I was sick of getting pieced up by everyone else who just "got it," so I was determined to figure out exactly what I wasn't getting. I set up my phone to record myself in training. I compared it to professional boxers on my own and eventually found pros to emulate whose style was closest to my own. I didn't only train at the gym either; I set up a room in my house to practice basic techniques. I wrote down all my goals, and I wrote down detailed plans to achieve them, and I re-read them every day.

I had realized that waiting to "get it" might take forever. "Getting it" doesn't just happen after a while, it only happens when you make a concerted, organized, disciplined effort. All those other guys who were getting it had made that effort, in and out of the gym, and it was up to me to choose to do the same. The only thing I regretted was how much time I had wasted before realizing this. That's why I've written this book; to save you as much time and effort as possible so you can get on the road to where you want to be as quickly and efficiently as possible.

It was less than one more month later that I noticed some serious changes in my game. And it wasn't just me. The coach was starting to put me in against the new guys. And guess what? I wasn't just able to 'help' them *notice* their mistakes, I was able to genuinely help them *fix* those mistakes as quickly and easily as possible, because I had made an organized and conscious effort to do so myself. That's when I really fell in love with the idea of being a boxing trainer in my own right.

The Sweet Science

Boxing is one of the oldest and purest sports in the world. A lot of sports are a metaphor for fighting. Boxing *is* fighting. One of the earliest known historical depictions of boxing was on ancient Sumerian tablets over 4,000 years old. Boxing was also popular in ancient Egypt and was an event in the original Olympic Games in ancient Greece, over 2,500 years ago. The modern sport of boxing, with the modern standard 12 to 18-ounce boxing gloves, a boxing ring, and the other rules associated with the sport, began in the 1800s. The rules were thereafter known by their sponsor's name: The Marquess of Queensbury Rules.

The premise of boxing is simple: Two people enter a ring and exchange blows until one cannot continue or until time runs out and judges determine a winner based on who landed the more effective punches each round. Despite this deceptively simple and brutal premise, hundreds of years' worth of experience and history has created an art known as the "Sweet Science." Defeating your opponent requires more than strength; it requires guts, discipline, technique, and intelligence. The wealthiest boxer to ever lace up the gloves, Floyd Mayweather Jr., famously said, "He can have heart, he can hit harder, and he can be stronger, but there's no fighter smarter than me."

With all that history, the brutality, the demands on one's heart, soul, body, and mind, it's no wonder boxing is intimidating. Heavyweight world champion Vitaly Klitschko once famously said, "What's the difference between boxing and chess? In chess, nobody is an expert, but everybody plays. In boxing, everybody is an expert, but nobody fights." That's true right up until the 'expert' who never fights steps into the ring with an actually experienced boxer and tries to go a round. Suddenly the 'expert' is cured of their delusion, and they experience firsthand the massive gulf between fighting in their imagination and fighting in reality.

Mike Tyson at the absolute height of his ability and fearsome talents gave an interview to Charlie Rose in 1990. He said, "I fight for perfection." Charlie Rose asked the brash, young, supremely confident, undefeated world champion, "Do you achieve it?" Mike Tyson answered, "Nah! No one does, but we aim for it." Even Iron Mike, when he was undefeated and already regarded as having the potential to be among the greatest fighters of all time, didn't believe he or anyone else had achieved perfection. Boxing is *hard*.

But you probably already knew that; that's why you picked this book up in the first place. If you've started training already, you definitely know that. In your mind's eye, you picture a professional with years, probably decades, of training and incredible, natural gifts. In the gym, you see seasoned veterans and maybe spar with experienced amateurs. In the mirror, you see yourself, in contrast. Now you want to know what you can do about it.

About Me

My name is Andrew Hudson, and I am a boxing coach turned author. I have been coaching and studying psychology for years. I help everybody I can fulfill their potential, inside and outside of the ring. My personal focus has been on teaching beginners because when I was a beginner it was when I struggled most - having made every mistake possible, I feel qualified to help beginners avoid these mistakes and break their bad habits.

I am confident I can turn anyone into a competent, confident boxer and get them well on their way to whatever next steps they wish to pursue. I have spent years refining my training techniques, drills, and methodology to help men reach their goals as efficiently as possible. I got into coaching because I want people to be able to turn their lives around just as I did with regular boxing training.

Growing up, I always feared making mistakes, especially in front of others. This stopped me from trying things, boxing in particular. I loved watching boxing in my early years and dreamed of fighting in the ring, however, I didn't join a gym for many years. I was scared that the other boxers would bully me and I would never be good enough. Eventually, I forced myself through those gym doors and have never looked back, and although boxing has presented me with some of my highest highs and lowest lows, overall it is responsible for shaping me into the better man I am today.

My battle with low self-esteem became more difficult the longer I went without doing anything about it, the same relates to boxing. Boxing is tough and you will make mistakes, trust me I've been there, however many of these mistakes will go under the radar and turn into bad habits, the longer you wait to tackle your errors the harder it becomes to fix them. So, it is best to gain awareness of them now while you are getting started with boxing, this way you speed up the rate at which you progress with your boxing and fitness ability.

Why Boxing?

The benefits of boxing are incredible. There is no greater test of fitness than a boxing match and nothing that makes for a better all-around athlete than boxing training. There is also no greater test of spirit and guts. There is nothing sweeter than victory, not just victory over another person, but more importantly, victory over your own doubts, your own fears, and your own perceived limitations - knowing that your hard work paid off.

Training in boxing is not just a personal quest; it's also participating in a vital aspect of our culture and history. It's sharing an experience with millions of people over hundreds of generations, stretching back to our earliest and most ancient civilizations in a nearly unbroken line down to the present day. It's immersing yourself in a primal need; the need to overcome fear and pain, and the need to answer the question: When the chips are down, when your body is failing, when your mind is telling you to quit, when every part of you wants to give up, what will you do? For a boxer, the answer to this question is the meaning of life itself. I am here to help you find your own answer.

Boxing is great to get into because you can choose your own level of commitment. You can get started by simply shadowboxing in your own home while reading this book and perhaps watching some free instructional videos. Or you can move up just one level and try a boxing fitness class where you'll work a heavy bag with an instructor and a group of other students together. It's great exercise and fun. Finally, you could even join a professional fighting gym, learn how to really fight with a serious trainer and other students, and prepare yourself to enter amateur or even professional competitions.

When you make that kind of commitment, it's incredibly motivating, and it makes it so much easier to keep yourself in excellent physical condition when you have something so tangible you're training for. One of my coaches once told me that every time I felt like sitting on my couch or eating some kind of junk food, I should picture the next guy I'm going to fight working out in the gym, eating clean, and getting ready to punish me.

Boxing doesn't discriminate; everyone can get benefits from it at any level. You can make a lot of progress on your own, and you can enjoy that progress with lifelong friends made in the gym. Boxing builds camaraderie and trust. It gives you something to live for beyond just making some money and buying some stuff, and it gives you something to train for beyond just some vague idea of being healthy. Nietzsche famously said, "A man who has a why can bear almost any how." Boxing can be your 'why.'

This Guide

In this book, we start from the very basics. In Chapter 1, we'll begin with an overview of what makes a great boxer and great student of boxing while laying out in step-by-step detail how to achieve whatever goals you have. In Chapter 2, we'll tackle the first and most common boxing mistake: self-doubt. In Chapters 3 to 7, we'll tackle each of the main technical aspects of boxing one by one, from stance and footwork to punching and defense. And finally, in Chapter 8 you'll learn the final key to improving your own game and technique as rapidly as possible. By the time you've finished this book, you will have the confidence and the know-how to accomplish your dreams, in *and* out of the ring.

Finally, throughout this guide, you will find multiple drills and exercises to aid with correcting your mistakes. Before you dive into them, please consult with a doctor and acknowledge the following:

- Do not attempt to exercise while unwell.

- Do not carry on exercising if you feel pain - if the pain doesn't calm, please tell your doctor.

- Avoid exercising after consuming alcohol or a large meal within the last couple of hours.

- If you take prescribed medication, check with your doctor to make sure it is okay to exercise.

- If you are in any doubt, go check with a doctor. It may be helpful to show the doctor the training routines you will partake in, if the doctor suggests for you not to partake in certain exercises there are always alternatives that will suit you.

I will not take any responsibility for any injuries.

The Boxing Training Handbook

A summary of essential boxing teachings, combining physical training techniques, practical drills, and key psychological lessons, in clear and concise points.

Follow the link below to download the handbook for **free**
www.subscribepage.io/boxingtraining

The Confidence Workbook

A hands-on guide containing 7 simple strategies designed to help you build self-esteem and develop confidence today.

Follow this link to get your **free** online copy
subscribepage.io/buildconfidence

1. Success Is No Accident

Boxing is undoubtedly one of the toughest sports to get into seriously. It has some unique challenges, but also many universal ones. Let's start by laying these challenges out so that we can then tackle and overcome them effectively. Then we'll get into what makes a great student of boxing and ultimately a good boxer. Having a clear idea in your mind of what you're aiming for is absolutely critical to hitting it. One thing to note though... It takes time to hit your target.

Improving Efficiently

So, you've hopefully started boxing, whether that's at home or at the gym. You know you are making many mistakes and you're not progressing with your boxing ability at the rate you want to. How can you improve more efficiently, or maybe it's more a question of how can you improve at all?

Knowing what you need in a general sense to become a great boxer is important to achieving your goals. The first step to overcoming a roadblock is to establish or reestablish, in your mind exactly where you're going. So, what makes a great boxer? There are two main aspects: the mental and the physical/technical. Any coach will tell you that the mental component is by far the most important to sharpen first. When you're in the right frame of mind and have the right attitude, everything else will follow naturally, but if you aren't, then everything will be a painful struggle. Therefore, if you've hit a roadblock, or if you just find it hard to get started, working on your mental game is usually the best place to start.

Improving Your Mental Game

Becoming a great boxer is a lot like becoming great at anything; it will take patience, determination, hunger, openness, and discipline. These are all traits that anyone can work on and improve, so don't think that this list is in any way exclusionary. Nobody starts out mentally perfect any more than they start out physically perfect; strengthening your mental game is a matter of directed effort over time, the same as everything else. Let's go over some common techniques that have worked for me and for tons of professional boxers and athletes of all kinds over the years.

Setting Clear Objectives

Understanding how to set your objectives properly makes achieving them way easier and more efficient. Setting good objectives for boxing is crucial because it provides a clear roadmap for growth, helping you identify where you currently are and where you want to go. This is the same for your personal development, it is a lifelong journey, and without clear objectives, it's easy to drift aimlessly without making meaningful progress. So, how do you set clear objectives?

- Be specific. You need to know exactly what you're aiming for. It's not enough to say "I want to be a good boxer;" you have to know exactly how good you want to be and why. Be specific about what you want; remember the old target shooter's adage: "Aim small, miss small". For example, instead of wanting to be a good boxer, you could strive to complete 3 rounds of sparring without getting knocked down.

- Ensure you can measure your progress. Being able to measure every little step on the way helps give the motivation and discipline to stay moving toward that progress. Being able to break your long-term objectives down into small, measurable steps makes achieving them much more probable.

- Your objectives need to be achievable. Ensure they are fully under your own control and not dependent on any kind of luck or outside circumstance and make sure it's something that comes down to a series of personal choices on your own part. Setting an objective that can be derailed by bad luck or other things outside of your control isn't always a bad thing, but it can be a trap that demotivates you when bad luck strikes, so bear that in mind.

- Your objectives need to be calibrated to the correct level of difficulty for where you are when you set them. If you are somebody who struggles to finish running the length of a 10k, then setting yourself a goal to run a sub 50-minute 10k in a month is very unrealistic, wouldn't you agree? Although, it is good to set challenging goals to push yourself, don't get carried away and fall into the trap of setting yourself harder goals to ones you can't even finish now.

- All of your goals have a set time period over which they should be achieved. Goal setting generally happens over three broad time frames: long-term goals, which should take up to three to five years; medium-term goals that build toward long-term goals and should take up to one year, and short-term goals that build toward your medium-term goals and take up to one to three months. Making a schedule for your goals and referring back to that schedule frequently also helps with the measurable aspect of your goal setting and achievement.

With these pointers in mind, start with your long-term goals. Generally speaking, you should restrict yourself to things you can realistically accomplish within three to five years for your long-term goals because it's just too hard to know what you and the world will be like much beyond that. Of course, there's nothing wrong with having a whole-life goal or something like a "bucket list," but anything that you cannot realistically achieve within the next five years is more accurately termed a 'dream' than a goal for most people. Dreams are wonderful and useful things to have; they tell you about your values and help set your long-term goals so that they will be aligned with your values.

Once you've set your long-term goal for boxing, it may, for example, be to win an amateur or professional bout, you can begin to think about the medium-term goals you need to accomplish to build toward that. If your goal is to win an amateur fight, perhaps the first medium-term goal to work toward would be to get your physical conditioning down to the point that you can easily box for a whole standard amateur bout, which would be either three 3-minute rounds for men or four 2-minute rounds for women. Other goals along that line would be to get to the point where you can reliably score points against some of the best sparring partners in your gym or reliably defend yourself and limit the number of points they can score against you.

Then, with your medium-term goals for boxing established, you can begin your short-term goals; the goals you can set to accomplish over the next month or so. At first this could be as simple as finding a good gym, creating a regular training and sleep schedule you can stick to for a whole month, and getting yourself on a proper diet that will propel you toward your long-term goals rather than holding you back. Creating the basic habits that will sustain your long-term vision is a great way to get yourself started along that path.

As you make these goals, make sure you write them down and put them somewhere you will see them every day. This could be written on paper and stuck onto your fridge or a bulletin board in your home somewhere convenient, or you could even type them out on your computer or smartphone and then take a screenshot and set them as your background. The point is to make sure that you are seeing your goals every day so you can remain focused on them over the long run. To-do lists have been of great help to me for the past decade!

Mistakes When Setting Objectives

- *Not being specific enough.*

- *Setting an objective that you cannot measure.*

- *Setting unrealistic objectives, especially in the beginning.*

- *Setting objectives that are dependent on others or other items out of your control.*

- *Mistaking someone else's objective for your own.*

- *Ignoring conditioning.*

- *Unrealistic expectations of the time and commitment it will take to achieve the objective.*

- *Skipping or ignoring the objective that should be set first (diet, sleep, gym location, etc.)*

- *Moving on to the next set of objectives without effectively achieving the first set.*

- *Not reviewing your objectives.*

Staying Organized and Focused

Once you've got your goals written and posted up somewhere, don't expect your goals to come to you, you need to work towards them with a strong plan. The next thing to do is to create a daily to-do list, which can be done using any notepad software on your smartphone or with a simple little paper notebook you can carry around in your pocket or bag every day. Every night as part of your bedtime routine, check over your to-do list for the next day. Is it complete, or are there things you need to add to it? In what order are you going to get everything on the list done? When are you going to start it and how long will it take to finish? When you've finished it, how will you reward yourself? Taking a minute or two each day before you go to sleep to check over this list has many benefits.

The most obvious benefit is that it will help you stay focused and organized which helps you avoid wasting any time. The next morning when you wake up, your day is already nicely planned out, so you can get right to it instead of wandering around wasting time in a bit of a fog as you gradually wake up and then begin making your plans. There is another even deeper and more important benefit, though: having this to-do list finished before you go to sleep is a great stress and anxiety reducer. One of the biggest sources of anxiety is simply the unknown and not knowing what you're going to do tomorrow is a big unknown. Getting rid of that unknown and replacing it with a plan for the day that will move you toward your goals and includes a nice small reward for yourself at the end, relieves all that anxiety. That in turn will help you sleep better and wake up more easily the next morning.

You can also set up to-do lists that will contribute towards your main goals, just writing down what you have to do to progress towards your main goals will help you maintain that momentum you have going on and keep you focused.

Mindfulness Meditation

The utility of meditation has long been known to Eastern Martial Artists, and most Eastern styles and schools of martial arts incorporate meditation sessions as a critical part of their daily training regimen. For whatever reason, Western martial arts like boxing have been slower to pick up on this as an essential part of a regular training regimen, but increasingly more trainers and gyms are catching on. If you incorporate mindfulness meditation into your regular training regimen, you will start to see the benefits very quickly, and it will even give you a nice advantage over anyone else who does not.

- *The basic practice of mindfulness meditation is to pick a nice, quiet, comfortable spot.*

- *Disconnect yourself from the world for a set amount of time.*

- *At first, 15 minutes is fine, but as you become more proficient, you may want to go for longer periods.*

- *During this time, you want to put away your phone and not allow yourself to be interrupted or disturbed by anyone or anything.*

- *As you begin, try to focus on a single, simple thought, image, or mantra.*

- *It could be something like counting slowly in your mind up to 10 and then back down again to one, repeatedly.*

- *Or it could be visualizing a leaf in a forest, falling from a tree, landing in a stream, and floating down the stream peacefully.*

- *Or it could be a mantra of gratitude, thinking of something you are grateful for and focusing on being grateful for that thing.*

- *In the context of training for boxing, imagining yourself throwing a perfect punch or combination can be another great focal point.*

- *Whatever it is, keep it very simple, try to clear your mind, and focus on nothing but that for as long as you can.*

What you will immediately begin to notice is that it's literally impossible. Intrusive thoughts will continually pop into your mind and distract you from the simple thought, image, or mantra you are trying to stick to. You will notice that this is completely beyond your control, and at first, that sensation may feel frustrating or irritating. When I tried this for the first time, the only thing that popped into my head was "What on earth am I doing?".

The real practice of mindfulness meditation is to accept that you are not your intrusive thoughts, that you have no control over them, but that you can acknowledge them, allow them to pass, and return yourself and your attention back to your focus point. As you practice this process of focusing your attention, inevitably losing it as intrusive thoughts arise, then noticing that you've lost focus, calmly dismissing the unwanted thoughts, and refocusing, over and over again, you will gradually start to experience the benefits:

- *The first thing you will notice is that you gain the ability to observe intrusive thoughts more quickly and easily and then dismiss them more quickly and easily.*

- *As you improve this ability, you will start to notice that you can begin to do the same with intrusive emotions and feelings; for example, the frustration and irritation you might have felt when you first noticed that it was impossible to focus on one simple thing for more than seconds at a time.*

- *As you practice mindfulness meditation, some of this ability will gradually carry over to the rest of your day as well.*

- *This will help you not only stay focused on important tasks, but it will also help you maintain your desired emotional state of mind.*

- *Masters of mindfulness meditation still get annoyed, angry, frustrated, scared, and so on, just like anyone else; but whereas a normal person might suffer from anger for hours over some unfortunate incident, after becoming a regular practitioner of mindfulness meditation they may be able to let go of that anger in seconds and then refocus their attention on solving the problem productively rather than self-destructively lashing out or stewing in anger pointlessly.*

This is extremely useful for any kind of combat martial art as well, including boxing. The ability to dismiss distracting thoughts and unwanted emotions and sensations drastically increases your ability to train effectively and to handle yourself skillfully in a real match as well. This took me a real while to get somewhere with, but I believe that meditation has helped me take control of my thoughts and emotions which help me channel that into boxing and achieving my goals.

As you increase in mastery over mindfulness meditation, you will find you can not only improve your focus and emotional control, but you can even reduce the amount of mastery that physical pain has over you. It's possible to notice the pain as nothing more than just another intrusion; just another unwanted sensation that you can calmly acknowledge, then dismiss, to refocus yourself on the simple task at hand, whether that's to finish your workout, or finish the round strong with point-scoring techniques.

Improving Your Physical Game

As you work on the above advice for improving your mental game, you'll find it much easier to get down to the job of improving the physical mechanics of your boxing game. For most of the rest of this book, I'll be breaking down how to do that, technique by technique, in the most efficient ways possible:

Stance

- The first technical part of any new boxer's game to get down is the stance.

- The stance is the starting point from which all other techniques flow.

- A good stance makes everything else you do easier, and a poor stance makes it harder.

- However, stances are also a lot like fingerprints; everyone is slightly different, tailored to their own physique and strengths.

- Settling into your own ideal stance cannot be done with a simple one-size-fits-all approach.

Footwork

- The next technical aspect is the footwork.

- Good footwork is essential for both offense and defense.

- The boxer with the better footwork is the boxer who will control the range properly and put themselves into a position to throw better, harder punches with a better chance of scoring.

- At the same time, they won't allow their opponent to get into a position to throw good punches back.

- Good footwork is rarely noticed by casual fans and observers of boxing, but whenever you see one boxer generally landing more punches than the other one, a discrepancy in footwork is often one of the primary reasons for that.

- Once you know what to look for, you can often see who's going to land a punch and who's going to miss before the first punch is thrown just by looking at their feet.

Punching

- After tackling your stance and footwork, we'll work on the meat of boxing: the punching.

- Punching will get a whole lot easier when the stance and footwork are right, but while good punches start from the feet, you still need your whole body to finish the punch, right down to the knuckles.

- And apart from the physical mechanics of punching, there's a ton of strategy to choosing your punches and setting them up with combinations, faints, and anticipating your opponent.

Defense

- Finally, we'll look at the defensive game, which is just as important as offense.

- Blocking, parrying, slipping, and ducking inside are all-important defensive techniques.

- Defensive moves provide protection.

- They prevent the opponent from scoring.

- Defense is used to set up counters to catch an opponent off guard.

- With proper defense, you will land better, cleaner shots of your own.

Throughout the book, identifying and correcting common mistakes will be emphasized. Knowing the basics is one thing; executing them properly in live sparring or a real match is another. The goal of this book is to help take you from knowledge to execution by helping you identify where your execution is falling flat and giving you tips and tricks for training to clean up those stubborn little errors and bad habits that are holding you back.

Don't Fear Your Mistakes

The final important point I want to make in this chapter is to never fear your mistakes. Fearing your mistakes is the only real mistake you can make. Fearing your mistakes leads to one of two equal and opposite problems:

- The first is that you are so fearful of your mistakes that you don't even try anything, or immediately give up on yourself as soon as you make your first mistake or hit your first roadblock or setback. This mindset is self-defeating.

- The second problem is caused when you're less consciously aware of your fear of mistakes, but it's still there, deep down. That subconscious fear causes you to ignore your own mistakes and keeps you from being consciously aware you're even making them, in order to protect your own ego from having to grapple with your imperfections. This can make you feel good about yourself for a little while, but sooner or later you may want to do something like spar with someone that really knows what they're doing. Your subconscious can't protect you anymore. and all the mistakes you've been making without realizing it will get exposed, one way or another.

Because these problems can be the most insidious for any serious, complicated, long-term pursuit, including boxing, the whole next chapter is devoted to learning to let go of your fear of mistakes. The biggest key to improvement and ultimate success is to stop fearing mistakes and failure, and instead, to go cheerfully and confidently in search of your own mistakes, to find them, thank them, and then correct them, one by one, getting ever closer to greatness every day. Don't expect boxing success overnight. Boxing is a lifelong quest for improvement, but it's worth it, and the rewards of the journey will come commensurately with the effort you put into it.

2. The Most Common Mistake

There is a famous story about Socrates, the ancient Greek philosopher and a much sought-after teacher in his day. As he was out shopping in the market, minding his own business, a nobleman appeared with his son to ask Socrates to teach him. Socrates could see that the boy was not terribly interested in being there, and sent them away, saying he was too busy. The next day, the nobleman and his son came to Socrates at his home and again, they asked Socrates to teach the boy. Socrates could see the boy was still not very interested in learning and again sent them away. On the third day, the boy came alone and again asked Socrates to teach him.

This time, Socrates asked the boy, "What is it you want me to teach you?"

"To be wise," said the boy simply.

"Fine," said Socrates, "then come with me."

Socrates led the boy to the shoreline, and then walked into the water until it was above his knees. He beckoned the boy to follow him into the water. Nervously, the boy did as he was told and came to stand beside Socrates with the water up to his waist. Then Socrates told the boy to put his head under the water for as long as he could. So, the boy did it, for a few seconds, then came up for air.

"What did you want while you were under the water?" asked Socrates.

The boy looked unsure, and eventually said, "To be wise."

Socrates told the boy to put his head under the water again, for longer. So, the boy tried again and managed a few more seconds. Again, Socrates asked the boy what he wanted while he was under the water, and again the boy answered.

"To be wise."

So, Socrates told the boy to try a third time, but this time when the boy gave up and tried to raise his head again after just a few more seconds, Socrates held his head underwater. The boy thrashed and tried to raise his head, but Socrates didn't let him move. Finally, after several more seconds, Socrates let the boy go, and he came back up gasping desperately for breath.

When the boy finally recovered, Socrates asked him again, "When you were under the water, what did you want?"

This time, the boy answered, "I only wanted air."

Socrates nodded, and said, "When you want to be wise as much as you want to breathe then you may become wise."

Certainly, a far harsher lesson than anyone should feel comfortable giving in the present day, but the story illustrates its point: The only way to become great at something is for your desire for greatness to overpower every other thought, feeling, and need that will distract you along the way.

There are going to be many such thoughts and feelings, but perhaps the most insidious is doubt, especially self-doubt. The greatest mistake that most new boxers make is doubting themselves. Doubting yourself is common because it's so easy to do, and once you start, it very quickly becomes a self-fulfilling prophecy. The more you doubt yourself, the worse you'll actually do. As Mihaly Csikszentmihalyi so eloquently describes in *Beyond Order and Anxiety,* it's impossible to enter the zone, the flow state, if your self-doubt is paralyzing you.

The Antidote to Doubt

It's one thing to know that self-doubt is bad; it's another thing to overcome it. After all, if you know you suck at boxing, how can it be possible to do anything but doubt yourself? And if you're new at boxing, surely knowing that you suck is better than willful deception. Isn't doubting yourself only rational at this point? Trying to convince yourself that you're awesome when you're clearly not isn't going to magically make you awesome. "Fake it till you make it" is a common refrain but not one that applies to something as technically and objectively difficult as boxing. The consequences of poor boxing skills cannot be avoided by 'fakery' once you're actually sparring with a competent boxer.

The important thing to understand is that you are not just your boxing skills today. You are also your boxing skills yesterday, and last week, and last month. Equally importantly, you are your boxing skills tomorrow, next week, next month, and five years from now. If you restrict your view of yourself to only a snapshot of what you are *right now,* you are missing the holistic view of everything you have accomplished in your life so far and everything you could accomplish for the rest of your life. That's almost everything!

Of course, it's only rational to have a realistic view of your boxing skills today, and as a new boxer, yes, those skills are poor compared to what they could be with dedication over time. That does not have to translate to self-doubt though; understanding how far you have to go to reach your goals can be a motivating and empowering feeling.

The real source of self-doubt is not the doubt you have about your present abilities, but rather the doubt that the effort you put into improvement will ever pay off. That's the real doubt that you need to be extra careful to nip in the bud. Doubt about whether putting effort into something will be worthwhile is what stops people from putting in enough effort to ever find out. It's very hard to tackle a difficult task if you don't believe you'll ever accomplish it or think it won't be worth it, even if you eventually do.

The best way to overcome this self-doubt consciously is to remember the sentiment expressed in the old chestnut, "Aim for the moon, so that even if you miss, you'll end up among the stars." When you set out to formulate long-term goals that will require years of effort and discipline to attain, that is an act of faith. You do so, understanding consciously or not, that you might not accomplish your goals. You might fail at them outright, or, more likely, you might decide that achieving them is not worth the cost you're paying and decide to aim at something else more worthwhile. These are all reasonable and rational thoughts to have. However, what is irrational and unhelpful is to then draw the conclusion that pursuing a challenging, long-term goal is not worth the effort at all because of the chance that you might not succeed and might ultimately decide is not worth that effort.

The reason that the only rational thing to do is pursue challenging goals regardless of the fact that you might fail or change your mind is that committing to the pursuit of a challenging goal is the only way to find out what you're truly capable of. If you dream of becoming a world champion boxer, you'll never know if that's what you're capable of or if that's what you truly want out of life until you make a real commitment to try. More importantly, though, no matter whether you succeed or fail at becoming a world champion, you will ultimately not regret whatever effort you put into it.

Nobody who aimed at greatness honestly and completely has ever regretted that aim, even if they didn't succeed in exactly the ways they initially dreamed. What you'll find when you talk to happy and successful people is that often what they ultimately succeeded most at is not what they initially set out to do. However, all the effort they put into their first pursuit was still extremely valuable in tangentially helping them accomplish what they ultimately did.

Setting a challenging objective is never a terrible idea - depending on the goal it may stretch how achievable or realistic it is but at the end of the day if you can make some real solid progress towards that challenging goal, that should rid your mind of doubt and help you with future goal setting and working towards goals.

The real antidote to self-doubt is *faith*. That faith doesn't have to be the kind of irrational faith that somehow magically all your goals will definitely come true no matter what. The only faith you need is the faith that all *your efforts will be rewarded*, one way or another. Either you'll find out that you really are cut out to be a champion, or a great trainer or coach, or just that you'll win an amateur bout to prove to yourself that you can. Or, somewhere along the way, you'll find out something else is even more important to you. But what you will invariably find is that once you start out on a dream, as long as you pursue it honestly and diligently to the best of your ability, either that dream will come true, or you'll find chances to trade up, not down. You'll find something better to do, not be forced to settle for less. All the effort you put in and the experience you gain will be of incredible value for the rest of your life, whether you accomplish what you first set out to do or whether you find something even better to aim at along the way. The people who are tormented by regrets at the end of their life are the people who didn't try when they had the chance because they doubted themselves.

How to Stay Mentally Strong

Having a clear long-term goal and rational faith in achieving it is a critical foundation for mental strength, but a foundation isn't everything. There are still going to be mental challenges to overcome every day just as there will be physical and technical ones. Here is a quick mental game help list to keep you at your best over the long haul.

Regulate Your Self-Talk

Self-talk is the inner monologue you have going on inside your own mind all the time. If you notice it turning negative and having thoughts like, "I'm not good enough to do this," or "This is too hard for me," or "I'm a terrible boxer," or anything of that nature, you need to get those thoughts out of your head. Try to interrupt them immediately, as soon as you notice them, and then try to cancel them out with positive self-talk equivalents, like, "I will get this with a little more effort," or "I'm getting better all the time." Later, when you're meditating or having a cooldown, or otherwise relaxing, you can revisit these thoughts in full, being introspective about where they're coming from and how useful they really are to accomplishing your goals and fulfilling your vision of who you really want to be.

With practice and discipline, you can get rid of negative self-talk that weakens you and becomes a self-fulfilling prophecy, and once you've done that, it's almost like removing training weights and seeing how fast and how far you can really run.

If you are somebody with more of a negative mindset who doesn't have the voice in their head telling you that you can do it, then I suggest you start to put those thoughts in your head. You have to believe in yourself if you truly want to smash a goal, so practice telling yourself "I will complete this workout" or whatever short-term goal you have in mind. There are so many ways of motivating yourself with self-talk, for myself, I like to compare how well I am doing with friends to get me in a competitive mindset. Maybe something you can try.

Practice Optimism and Positivity

An optimistic viewpoint makes success much more likely than a pessimistic one. The outcomes we get in life are in many ways often the results of what we already believed would happen. An optimist who believes in themselves and their chances of success will be more likely to push through difficulties and ultimately achieve what they already believed they could. Likewise, a pessimist who is full of doubts not only about themselves but about the 'fairness' of the world as such, is much more likely to give up at the first sign of trouble if they even bother to try anything difficult in the first place.

Optimism, of course, doesn't guarantee success in everything you do every time; nothing can do that. But optimism doesn't mean blind faith that you, everyone else, and everything is perfect; optimism is really just the belief that if you work hard enough for long enough, you'll get a much more positive outcome than just giving up and blaming yourself or the world for your failure. Also, being optimistic and positive generally makes you a more pleasant person to work with than the alternative, and that makes it more likely that your coaches, teammates, and others will be willing to help you through any tough times you may encounter.

Reward Yourself Wisely

Boxing, like life, is challenging. It takes hard work, discipline, and endurance. One way to make tackling a difficult task easier is by having something nice to look forward to at the end of it. Hence, reward yourself wisely. There are three aspects to this. Firstly, don't forget to reward yourself when you've done great work. Don't be such a harsh taskmaster that you deny yourself all positive rewards even when you clearly deserve it. Let go of guilt over pleasures you've earned.

Secondly, with that being said, try to reward yourself with responsible pleasures. Any fighter trying to drop a few pounds to make a certain weight class would be very foolish to reward themselves for going on a run with a double fudge ice cream shake! A reward by definition doesn't have to directly contribute to your long-term goals, it just has to make you feel good about the progress you've made; but at the same time, don't reward yourself with something that's going to erase the progress you've made.

Finally, don't reward yourself *before* you've actually accomplished what you're rewarding yourself for. This is sort of like the admonition against bragging about the goals you've set. It's fine to tell trusted friends and family that you've set tough goals for yourself but do it with the mindset that doing so helps you hold yourself accountable to those goals; otherwise, if you're just enjoying praise from them for having goals, you're getting the reward before the accomplishment. Likewise, if you sit down to enjoy an hour or two of video games before a training session because you have every intention of doing that training session afterward, well, maybe when the time comes your mind finds a convenient excuse to put off training; that's a whole lot easier for your mind to do when you've already enjoyed the reward you promised yourself before having to do any of the actual work.

Create an Environment That Enables Success

One of the most important aspects of your life is your environment; it's what surrounds you every day from the time you wake up to the time you go to sleep. Controlling your environment to create factors that will contribute to your success and eliminate obstacles is one of the most efficient ways to help yourself accomplish your goals. Here are a few quick tips to make sure your environment is working with you, not against you:

- *Make sure your bedroom helps you sleep well. Try to have a cool, dark room at night, and remove sleep distractions like a computer or laptop, a TV, or even your phone. All you need is your notebook with your to-do list and an alarm clock.*

- *Stock your kitchen with healthy foods and remove junk foods. The time to resist temptation is when you're shopping, so don't go shopping when hungry! As long as there's only healthy food in your home, it's way easier to eat healthily.*

- *Make your home inspiring and beautiful. Put up nice pictures, play energizing music, put up your goals in plain sight, and surround yourself with things that will encourage your success every time you see them. If possible, put up a heavy bag and/or speed bag, a big mirror for shadow boxing, a place for jumping rope, and similar training tools to help you stay sharp and increase your practice time.*

- *Associate rooms of your house with different tasks. For example, have a room for studying, a room for exercise, only use your bedroom for rest and so on. You may not have enough rooms in your house for this, so dedicate areas of space in your house to these tasks. It is beneficial to do this because your brain begins to associate certain areas with certain tasks which makes it easier for you to get in that flow state.*

Mentally Adding to Your Training

Boxing, like most any sport, can be extremely physically demanding, so there is a hard physical limit on how much you can effectively train. However, great boxers, like all great athletes, don't limit themselves to just physical training. Apart from the hard physical work in the gym, there's a lot you can do outside of the gym to stay mentally sharp. Here are a few common things anyone can do to maximize their improvement even after they've hit their physical limits:

- *Take notes after every session: What did you learn today? What are you struggling with? What questions do you want to ask your trainer or coach next session? What are you improving at? Try to list positives along with every problem so that you don't fool yourself into thinking you're stagnating or stuck in a rut when you aren't. The mere act of writing is important; it engages a different part of your mind which makes the lessons more memorable and meaningful.*

- *Visualize yourself going through techniques even when you aren't physically doing them. Visualization is a powerful tool to mentally prepare yourself for physical success; it primes your mind and improves reaction times and reduces the negative impact of unexpected distractors. Don't just visualize yourself raising your hands in victory, though; visualize yourself getting every detail of a specific technique right. Try to remember and incorporate the advice of a coach or in this book about how to do every technique correctly as you visualize. There's no time to do this kind of thinking at the moment, so use visualization to do it in advance.*

- *Use video aids. Watching videos on yourself, your opponent if possible, and great boxers you want to emulate is a technique as old as the video itself. There's an incredible wealth of such videos for free on YouTube, so this has never been easier. And, if possible, having someone record you while sparring can give you an outside perspective on what you look like in the moment, which can help you with your visualization techniques to target specific areas for improvement.*

- *Stress Inoculation Training. Exposing yourself to simulated stressful situations to reduce the impact of stress during actual fights. You need to make this a habit because if you don't develop your ability to handle stress then when you need to perform it is likely you will crumble. So incorporate drills that mimic fight conditions—such as high-pressure sparring or performing drills while fatigued—to build your mental endurance.*

- *Reaction Training with Cognitive Drills. Use tools like light reflex balls, reaction lights, or cognitive apps that test decision-making while moving. React to unpredictable stimuli and make fast decisions under physical exertion. Using exercises that combine physical and cognitive elements to improve reaction time and decision-making will be a great help to your offensive and defensive ability.*

- *Mental Recovery. Schedule regular mental breaks from training, engage in relaxing activities like walking or reading, and prioritize sleep for brain recovery. Recognize the importance of mental recovery as it helps reduce mental fatigue, keeps motivation high, and promotes long-term performance.*

Avoid Burnout

Burnout is one of the biggest threats to long-term success. Now that I've bombarded you with advice on how to inundate yourself with boxing improvement techniques, I want to make sure you don't turn around and burn yourself out! The burst of enthusiasm that usually begins major endeavors like success in boxing can all too easily burn itself out before success is achieved if you aren't careful. To avoid that, here are a few tips to help you combat burnout before it becomes a problem:

- *Maintain a few interests outside of boxing. You can improve in boxing to a fair degree without totally dedicating your life to it; but even if you do decide to totally dedicate your life to boxing, that doesn't mean you have to totally eliminate all other outside interests and relationships. Having at least one rest day each week dedicated to something outside of boxing helps recharge your mental energy and keeps you fresh for all the other days you are dedicating to boxing.*

- *Stay connected to nature, especially if you live in a big city. Humans are naturally evolved to be connected to nature, and therefore, being exposed to the natural world from time to time is essential for maintaining our mental health and balance. Try to follow the 20-5-3 rule: 20 minutes walking in a park at least 3 times a week, 5 hours a month in a natural environment, and 3 days a year camping without modern technology. This minimum exposure to nature can help combat burnout in boxing or in any other long-term discipline.*

- *Revisit your long-term goals periodically. Remind yourself why you're doing what you're doing and why it's worth it. One of the first tips my driving instructor gave me was to focus my vision on a point far away from the front of my car—all the way down to the end of the road I was on if possible. When I did that, my hands became much steadier on the wheel; when I looked just in front of the car, my hands were shaky and constantly making little micro-adjustments to stay straight. Accomplishing goals works the same way; stay focused on your long-term goals to stay steady. If you only focus on the immediate, you'll be easily distracted and constantly make unnecessary micro-adjustments.*

- *Be mentally prepared to take failures, setbacks, and plateaus in stride. Of course, we all hope that we'll succeed at everything quickly and easily while continually and regularly improving until we accomplish our ultimate vision of success, but realistically, we also have to be aware that life basically never works like that. Everyone is going to hit a failure, have a setback, or have to endure a plateau—a time where it seems like progress isn't coming at all—at some point. We don't know when they will come or what they will look like, but we know they're going to happen somehow, someway, sooner or later. Accept this reality and be prepared to keep pushing past it regardless. Forgive yourself for mistakes, learn from setbacks, and endure the plateaus with stoicism. Progress is never a straight line, but if you maintain your wise optimism and discipline, you'll get to where you wanted to go—or somewhere even better.*

- *Enjoy some popular boxing media, too. There are so many great inspirational boxing movies out there, like the Rocky and Creed series, Cinderella Man, Ali, The Hurricane, and great boxing documentaries like When We Were Kings, that can help you recharge your mental batteries and remind you why you got into boxing in the first place after a tough day or two.*

3. Your Sloppy Stance

Now that we've talked about the real foundation of boxing success, your mental game, it's time to move on to the real foundation of technical boxing skills: your stance. Having a great boxing stance is the first and most important thing you need to master in order to have any success in the ring, but it's far from easy to do so. There are many problems in figuring out your perfect boxing stance because boxing stances are a bit like fingerprints—no two are exactly the same. Everyone has a slightly different body and a slightly different boxing 'temperament' so finding your ideal stance is something that will take some time. Keeping that ideal stance while in a fight, and properly incorporating it with your footwork, punches, and defense is where the real mastery shows through.

Finding Your Stance

Your stance is made up of several individual components, and we'll tackle them one at a time, from the ground up. As you read this section, try to find a good place where you can assume a stance and see yourself in a mirror as you move around a little bit. Your stance is the position from which all other techniques will ideally begin, so it's critical that you get it right. As the old adage goes, "well begun is half done."

Your stance is the first thing any trainer or coach will look at to determine whether you have any boxing skills at all, and the first thing they will teach any beginner, so you should already know what a decent stance looks and feels like. Just to get it out of the way, we'll go over a quick checklist of what a proper stance looks and feels like.

- Foot placement: *Your feet need to be shoulder width apart. As far as foot placement goes, your front foot should be pointed forward and your back foot should be angled 45 degrees to your front foot. The front foot should be planted on the ground, with the majority of the weight on the ball of the foot. For the back foot, the heel should be slightly lifted so you can improve your* mobility. The weight distribution between each foot should be equal.

- Knees: *Your knees should be slightly bent, neither locked straight nor bent too deeply.*

- Hips: *Your hips should be turned diagonally relative to the opponent, creating an angle for your whole upper body, to your shoulders. You should be bent very slightly at the waist to compensate for your slightly bent knees, but still standing with your back straight.*

- Shoulders: *Your shoulders should be in line with your hips, so that your back isn't twisted. Your shoulders should also be in line with your knees. Don't hunch your shoulders, keep them loose.*

- Head: *Tuck your chin down, keeping it even with or below the tops of your shoulders, so that your forehead is towards the opponent, protecting your chin and neck. Keep your mouth closed, firmly gripping your mouthguard, and breathe through your nose as much as possible. Keep your eyes on your opponent at all times; even when ducking away from or under punches, always try to maintain a clear line of sight with your opponent.*

- Arms and Hands: *Keep your elbows pointed down and tucked tight to your body. Your rear power hand should be held very close to the side of your chin, just below eye level, while your front hand should be held out in front of your face a few inches away from your nose. Some trainers also teach a style where the front hand is held lower, more protecting the body while your front shoulder and rear hand protect your head; both styles have their pros and cons and both can be found at the professional level.*

- Weight Distribution: *Your center of gravity, which is right above and in the middle of your hips, should be in the center of your stance. About 55-60% of your weight should be on your back foot, and all the weight on both feet should be on the front of your feet, not your heels.*

Identifying Stance Mistakes

- Not finding the coaches and trainers that are experienced with your natural stance. (especially if you are a southpaw boxer)

- Having too wide of a stance - *will hinder your foot movement and burn excess energy.*

- Having too narrow of a stance - *will have a negative impact on your balance, therefore, hindering your punching power as well as your ability to evade or deflect punches from your opponent.*

- Knees too bent - *this will drain excessive energy and cause you to give up height and reach, putting you at a disadvantage.*

- Knees too straight - *this will reduce your punching power and slow down your movement.*

- Stood aligned perpendicular to your opponent - *this will leave you open to hooks and your dominant hand will then be too far away to effectively counter.*

- Aligned facing straight onto your opponent - *this will leave you vulnerable to straight punches and body shots as well as reducing the load up and power potential of your dominant hand.*

- Not keeping your elbows down and in - *will leave your sides vulnerable.*

- Not keeping your hands up - *will leave your chin and face vulnerable to your opponent. Although some boxers like Roy Jones Jr. or Muhammed Ali would purposefully lower their hands to draw their opponents into their counterpunching traps, this is not a good strategy for beginners.*

- Lifting your chin upward - *will create the opportunity for your opponent to hit you with a knock-out punch.*

- Keeping your lead hand too far forward - *you'll expend more energy hanging it out there and it will hinder the speed at which you can load up and throw a jab.*

- Keeping both heels flat - *will hinder your movement.*

- Leaning forward - *you'll be doing your opponent a favor by leaning into their punches and giving them more power.*

Correcting Common Mistakes

Since the stance is quite literally the base of your entire boxing game, with any difficulty you're having in the ring, the stance is the obvious first place to look. Whether it comes to your movement, offense, or defense, everything starts and ends with a proper stance that is both well-balanced and emphasizes your natural strengths and boxing temperament.

Stance Mistake #1: Losing Your Stance

One of the most common errors is simply losing your stance. This is typically caused by moving around; you get out of your stance without consciously noticing it. To correct this error, what you want to be particularly aware of is to purposefully recover your stance properly after any kind of movement. No matter if you're moving forward or backward, ducking or slipping in place, or throwing punches, you want to get in the habit of immediately recovering your proper stance after every movement.

A simple drill to practice that helps you avoid losing your stance is to stand in front of a big enough mirror to see yourself, get into your proper stance, fix it in your memory, then get out of the stance.

- *Start by simply relaxing to a normal standing position, then get into your stance position. Do this 10 to 15 times to really fix it in your muscle memory.*

- *Then instead of simply relaxing, throw a few punches and then recover your stance. Again, do this 10 to 15 times.*

- *As you're doing this drill, focus on bringing your hands back to the proper position as quickly as possible, and if you're throwing proper, solid punches (more on this later) you'll be moving your feet, hips, and shoulders before your hands, so focus on recovering the correct position for each part of your body as quickly and accurately as possible.*

- *Finally, incorporate some movement; take a few steps forward, back, and sideways in both directions, add a few punches at the end, and then recover your stance after each movement.*

- *Do it slowly at first so you can ensure that after and between each step, your stance is correct. After doing this third version of the drill 10 to 15 more times, you have a nice 5-minute stance workout/drill you can incorporate into a daily warmup and cooldown routine.*

Stance Mistake #2: Going Flat-Footed

Once you've practiced recovering your stance between every movement, let's look at a few details that will ensure your stance is contributing to your movement, offense, and defense rather than hindering it. We'll go back again to tackling common potential errors from the ground up, so we'll start with the feet.

The most common error with your feet is being flat-footed. If you're 'flat-footed' that typically means that your weight is on your heels rather than the balls of your feet; especially the back foot, which should be carrying a bit more of your weight. When you're flat-footed your movement will be much slower because you need to first shift your weight to the balls of your feet to launch yourself forward or back; if you don't, you're just sort of 'falling' in one direction or another and letting gravity do most of the work, which is typical of a boxer who's tired and is one of the factors that makes tired boxers move more slowly.

The second problem with going flat-footed: If you plan to throw a punch with power, you must move your feet first, but if you're flat-footed, you will struggle to do this as your feet will be planted to the ground, which will reduce the speed and power of your punches.

One of the oldest drills in the boxing book for going flat footed is actually just skipping rope. It's impossible to skip rope flat-footed, so skipping rope for minutes on end builds up not just the muscle memory to stay on the balls of your feet at all times, but it also builds up the strength and conditioning to maintain that proper form for an entire match. Of course, you can practice the little hops and moving around on the balls of your feet without skipping rope but incorporating the rope can make it more interesting to maintain for a long period of time, and it may also have some benefits in improving your coordination. Tips for effectively skipping rope include:

- *Choosing a rope of the appropriate length for your height (standing on the center of the rope, the handles should reach around your armpits).*

- *Breathing through your nose instead of your mouth.*

- *Landing with your knees slightly bent and on the balls of your feet.*

- *Maintaining posture, don't round your back.*

- *Focusing on short, fast jumps (single jump and not a double bounce between rotations).*

- *Generating rope movement through your hands and wrists, not your arms and shoulders.*

There are a variety of styles and techniques ranging from beginner to advanced, so if one technique becomes too easy, level up:

- Basic jump rope: *one rotation, one small hop.*

- Double under: *basic jump rope but getting two rotations with the rope every hop.*

- Run in place: *running in place, the rope rotates between foot strikes.*

- Single leg jump rope: *basic jump but with only one foot.*

- Front to back or side to side: *basic jump, but with feet together move forward or backward between strikes, same idea with side to side movement.*

- Boxer skip: *incorporate your stance and footwork rhythm by shifting between your feet as you also rotate and jump over the rope.*

Stance Mistake #3: Hip and Shoulder Misalignment

Properly aligning your hips and shoulders is an essential part of both offense and defense. Make sure your hips and shoulders are in the same alignment, rather than your hips facing one angle and your shoulders in a different, offset angle. That will cause your back to be twisted, which is not just a little uncomfortable and awkward, but will also reduce your ability to properly load up your punches, quickly slip, or re-position in response to the opponent's punches and movements.

The proper way to adjust the alignment of your upper body relative to your opponent, whether you are simply moving and repositioning, throwing a punch, or executing a defensive technique, is to always begin with your feet, ankles, and knees. Your legs move to turn your hips, your hips turn your upper body, and your hips and shoulders stay in perfect alignment the whole time, while your shoulders remain over your knees. Turning your body properly is impossible if your weight is on your heels; you need your weight on the balls of your feet so your toes can easily change direction, which will then change the direction your knees are pointing, which then changes your hip and upper body's facing.

This mistake is often a result of fighters trying to save energy when fatigued. It can be very tiring to turn your body using your feet and knees to keep your hips and shoulders aligned, so fighters tend to just turn at the hips which misaligns their body. It's essentially the same problem already mentioned above, of being flat-footed.

Therefore, the best drill to correct this mistake is to repeat following a moving opponent, after you've already jumped rope to exhaustion, if you don't have a partner you could visualize this. That will not only help build up the conditioning needed to maintain proper technique but also reinforce your muscle memory to maintain proper technique even after you're already tired. Remember to start the movement with your feet.

Stance Mistake #4: Standing Too Square

Another big error of alignment is to be too square-on to your opponent; in other words, to have your whole upper body directly facing the opponent. In terms of defense, this just makes your body a bigger and easier target, and any straight punches they throw are going to land square and flush, giving them more power. In terms of offense, this removes the distinction between your front and power hands. Typically in boxing, your lead hand is used for quick jabs and occasional lead hooks with the main purpose being to strike quickly to take advantage of momentary opportunities or set up your power shots. Meanwhile, your rear hand is the power hand for delivering stronger blows that have the potential to stun or ideally knock out the opponent. If you stand square-on, you won't really have either a lead hand or a rear hand; they'll both be closer to equally quick and equally strong, meaning neither is really doing the job they're supposed to. Your lead hand will be slower, and your power hand will be weaker—that is not ideal.

Here is a staggered shadowboxing drill to reinforce a more angled, balanced stance and improve foot positioning, making it more natural to stay bladed (one shoulder leading) rather than square. Follow the instructions below:

- Start by establishing a correct boxing stance.

- Stand in front of a mirror to observe your stance. Begin by practicing basic movements like stepping forward and backward, as well as lateral (side-to-side) movements. Keep your stance staggered and maintain the angle of your feet as you move.

- Cue: Check that your shoulders and hips stay angled, with your lead shoulder slightly in front. If you notice yourself squaring up, reset and return to the bladed position.

- Start shadowboxing slowly, focusing on maintaining a proper stance throughout. Throw basic punches (jab, cross, hook) while paying attention to your foot positioning and body alignment. Focus on keeping your rear shoulder back and staying at an angle—don't allow your feet to drift closer together or square up.

- Work with a partner: Have your partner lightly tap at your gloves or shoulders with mitts or their hands. Move laterally, stepping to the side or pivoting to avoid being tapped. The goal is to keep your stance correct during movement. If you square up, your partner should stop the drill and have you reset your stance before continuing.

- Heel Tap Drill: Tie a string or place a marker on the floor to create a line for your lead heel to follow. Every time you move, ensure your lead heel stays in alignment with the line while your back foot stays staggered. This helps reinforce proper positioning and prevents you from inadvertently squaring up as you move.

Practice this drill daily for 10-15 minutes, incorporating it into your regular shadowboxing and footwork training. Gradually speed up the drill as you become more comfortable maintaining the correct stance.

Stance Mistake #5: Standing Too Perpendicular

As you may have guessed, the next error is the opposite of the previous; rather than being too square-on to your opponent, your shoulders are too in-line with your opponent. This creates equal and opposite problems in both offense and defense as being too square-on. While your body being in-line with your opponent makes it the smallest possible target for straight punches, it makes it a much more vulnerable target for hooks, especially hooks that come around your back and could land on your kidneys or ear, away from where your hands and arms can defend you and out of the line of sight, unless your head is already dramatically twisted, which also isn't good. As for offense, being totally in line with your opponent makes your front hand have zero room to load up, which makes it tough to throw with enough power for your opponent to even notice it, and it makes your rear hand have too far to go, making it harder to reliably land.

The most common source of these two kinds of errors, being either too square or too perpendicular to your opponent, is losing track of your facing after throwing a combination of punches, or after moving around a lot defensively to evade the opponent's punches. The more you move your body rapidly in a stressful moment, the easier it is to lose track of your correct body positioning and facing.

The typical drill to get your upper body alignment correct is to practice throwing 1-2 and 1-2-3-4 combinations (more on this in Chapter 5) in front of a mirror and observing your start and end positions while also paying attention to how your trunk feels. Your trunk is your chest, abdominals, back and pelvis in case you didn't know.

- *You want to have a bit of twisting as you're loading the punch, but you should feel your body untwist and completely align before and after each punch.*

- *You can also practice the defensive side of this with a partner, having them throw very light combinations that you slip and parry with hip and shoulder turns.*

- *The biggest training mistake many new boxers make that leads to this problem is just not doing it enough times.*

- *Many new boxers think that practicing the same combination five or ten times is plenty, then get bored and move on to the next technique they want to work on.*

- *If you really want to nail your technique, you should be aiming for at least 30 reps every time, and concentrating on getting every detail right with every rep. That's the kind of mental discipline you need to cultivate to see real improvement.*

Stance Mistake #6: Leaning Forward

Leaning forward in your neutral stance creates some big problems in both offense and defense. Leaning too far forward, also known as being "front-heavy," in your neutral position, causes you to be leaning into the opponent's punches as they come in, which adds to the power with which they land. At the same time, if you're already leaning forward when you've started to throw your own punches, you have that much less room to move as you throw, which reduces your own power and reach. You want to be leaning in just as your punch lands, so it lands with maximum power. If you're already leaning toward your opponent when your punches begin, it makes it easier for the opponent to judge your range and defend themselves.

The main source of the error of leaning forward too much is often being over-eager on the offense against a defensive opponent. A good defensive boxer that knows what they're doing can use this to their advantage by luring you into leaning forward too much, then capitalizing on your predictability to land counterpunches with the extra power of using your own body weight against you.

A good drill to avoid this mistake is to practice throwing combinations on a heavy bag or in front of a mirror and paying extra attention to returning to a neutral stance without leaning forward after each punch. Later on, when we talk about footwork, also remember this section, because the real key to pursuing a good defensive fighter without falling into their trap and leaning into them too much is always chasing with your feet first, not your upper body.

Stance Mistake #7: Leaning Backward

At the same time, if you're leaning away from the opponent in your neutral stance, you have much less room to move back when the opponent throws a punch, and nowhere to roll with the punch if it lands. That will cause you to lose balance and stumble backward or even get knocked down much more easily, which will cost you points with the judges. When it comes to offense, if you're leaning away from the opponent when you throw your punches, you'll have to move your whole body much more forward before you land the punch for it to have impact, which will either reduce your power or give the opponent that much more time to evade your punch.

The most common source of this error is in dealing with a very aggressive, offensive-minded opponent that is always coming forward and throwing combinations. After a while of moving backward, it's easy to start leaning back more and more without even realizing it.

- *A typical drill to practice finding your balance and avoiding leaning too far backward is to find your ideal stance in front of a mirror and then visualize punches from an opponent coming toward you.*

- *As they come toward you, your instinct is to lean back, away from the punches, so for each imagined punch, lean back a bit to either avoid the punch or "roll with it" as it lands, but then immediately recover your balance and return to your center point.*

- *If you don't, you'll find you have nowhere left to lean on the next visualized punch, so when it comes in, you have nowhere left to go to avoid it.*

- *At the same time, as you're avoiding the visualized punches and then coming back to your center point, also practice throwing a few punches of your own. Your imagined opponent will also lean away, so you have to lean forward to reach them and land with any kind of decent power.*

- *Again, after you lean forward, make sure you immediately come back and recover your center point. If you have a real training partner to work on this drill with, even better.*

- *Just make sure that you aren't actually landing punches on each other. You want to simulate the offensive and defensive exchanges without real contact so you're just focusing on getting and maintaining proper technique under some pressure, not actually getting hit.*

A key point to notice is that your feet remain still for this drill; you aren't practicing your footwork yet (we'll get to that in the next chapter), so the amount of actual upper body movement you're doing should be fairly subtle. Just a few inches backward or forward is enough lean and a shift of balance to create a big effect. If you're leaning much more than that, it's a bit too wild, uncontrolled, and unbalancing so you'll have to move your feet to 'catch' yourself, and that also wastes a lot of energy.

Intermediate Stance Mistake: The Stance Switch

The stance switch is a technique used by advanced boxers to set up powerful hooks and uppercuts. This technique is effective when you are within close range of your opponent, use it as the first move in a feint, punch, or block, or in the face of an advancing opponent. To initiate the switch from southpaw to orthodox or vice versa, the first movement is to push up with your front foot while simultaneously bringing your back foot forward. You will end up rotating your body, changing the way you are oriented toward your opponent.

Mistakes commonly encountered with the stance switch include making the initial movement a jump and spin, rather than a push and switch. You should not catch a lot of air with this movement and stay as close to the ground as possible. While thinking about the complicated footwork, there is a tendency to drop your guard, which will leave you open to attack.

Here is a drill to practice the stance switch properly. This is a powerful, explosive, and quick movement. You'll want to maintain focus on those aspects during the drill and don't forget to add your hook or uppercut at the end to finish off the movement.

- *A partner will be helpful in this drill. Have them circle around you and yell 'switch' at random times.*

- *Have your partner continuously change their distance to you as well and only perform the switch if they are within close range or moving into range.*

- *As you practice this drill, you'll need to pay attention to where your feet land each time you switch, making sure that they are landing within a proper stance. It is a wasted movement to jump switch if your feet land outside of your stance and you have to shuffle them around.*

I hope you can identify the mistake or mistakes you are making from this chapter and use the corrective drill to work on getting into that habit of holding your stance at every moment while punching the bag or sparring with an opponent. It may seem stupid that I am asking you to 'imagine' an opponent at times to help you with your stance errors, but believe me keep practicing using the advice I am giving to fix your mistakes and you will naturally hold your stance while moving and throwing punches.

4. Your Clumsy Footwork

Footwork is often the biggest difference between two boxers of different skill levels. Another way of putting it is that the majority of boxing matches are won and lost based on the difference in footwork. This may sound surprising to the casual fan of boxing or the average person because generally when we're watching a boxing match, we tend to focus on the punches thrown and landed, and it seems pretty obvious that whoever throws better punches will tend to be the guy that lands them more often with more power and ends up winning. The average, casual observer is rarely looking much at the feet in a boxing match. After all, nobody is going to throw any kicks; boxing matches are fought with the hands. However, more often than not, it is the position of their feet that determines who is going to be able to throw the better punches with more power and with a better chance of landing. Therefore, having better footwork is an essential part of actually winning any boxing match.

The Basics of How to Step and Move

The essence of footwork is stepping and moving safely, quickly, and efficiently without losing your stance. By looking in detail, you can break down a ton of little mistakes, but the broader, meta-mistake for beginners almost always boils down to some variation of losing your stance. This includes losing your balance, misplacing your feet, going flat-footed, getting 'lazy' or 'sloppy,' and wasting energy. These mistakes luckily can be corrected fairly simply, even on your own, with the proper drills and attention. We'll look at the basic movements needed for stepping in each of the cardinal directions first.

- Moving forward: *Move your front foot first, springing off the balls of your back foot.*

- Moving backward: *Transfer a bit more weight to your front foot so you can push off it, moving your back foot first.*

- Moving sideways: *Move the foot that's in the direction you want to move first, so you're always widening your stance before you narrow it. Avoid crossing your feet at all costs. Moving left shall result in you moving your left foot to the side first, before moving your right foot.*

Basic Rules of Movement

- *Keep your hands up and your chin lowered at all times.*

- *As you first start practicing these movements, you'll naturally want to look down at your feet, but once you've got the basics down, practice keeping your eyes up and on your opponent.*

- *The foot closer to the direction that you're moving in always moves first, so that your stance is slightly wide as you're moving, never narrower, and especially never crossing your feet.*

- *Your head follows your first foot to move and leads your other foot so that your balance is always properly centered, with a bit more weight on the back foot at the end of each movement.*

- *Don't twist your feet, your knees, your hips, or your back as you move; keep your proper orientation relative to the opponent, with special care to maintain this while moving sideways.*

- *Move with shorter steps when closer to the opponent; no more than one or two-foot lengths if in punching range. You can take bigger steps to save energy when out of punching range.*

- *Don't pick your feet up off the mat more than an inch or so as you move; conserve your energy and balance by 'sliding' your feet along or lifting them just barely enough to move.*

- *Don't step with your heel or ever go flat-footed; every step begins and ends on the balls of your feet.*

- *Bring your trailing foot up the same amount of distance that you moved your first foot; don't end with your stance either too wide or too narrow.*

- *Don't 'bob' your head up and down any more than is necessary; try to keep your head fairly level and balanced.*

- *Try to stay loose without being 'lazy' or 'sloppy.' If you're too tight and tense, you'll waste energy and actually slow your reflexes; but also avoid regressing to anything like your natural daily-life walking mechanics when in range of the opponent, which will be too slow and leave you unable to properly attack or defend.*

Basic Footwork Drills

The following basic footwork drills are great ways to work on getting the essential mechanics of footwork into your muscle memory and you could be doing these every day if you want to improve efficiently.

- *Of course, the first and most basic thing you'll want to do is just practice moving around forward, backward, and sideways while keeping in mind all of the technical details discussed previously.*

- *Doing this with a mirror or even recording yourself on a smartphone can help you notice mistakes that you can't feel.*

- *Once you're confident you can get the basic technical details right while moving around freely, the next thing to do is to find or make a straight line a few meters or yards long on the ground.*

- *Assume your neutral stance with the toes of your front foot and the heel of your rear foot on the line.*

- *Then simply practice moving forward and backward along the line while concentrating on not only properly maintaining your balance and all the technical details of your stance and movement, but also staying on the line, so your front toes and rear heel are landing in line.*

- *As said above, at first you'll want to look down at your feet as you do this, but you'll want to get to a point where you can move backward and forward a few steps without looking, and then look down to verify you're still on the line or very close to it.*

What you're really concentrating on improving here is your muscle memory and consistency to the point that you will be aware of your whole body's position and movement relative to your starting position without having to consciously think about it. As you improve, it should carry over to help you become better at maintaining relative position and distance to your opponent in the ring. A similar drill is to:

- *Make yourself a large rectangle of lines on the floor.*

- *Start by standing on one of the lines of the rectangle as above, but when you move up to the front corner of it, you then move laterally (sideways), keeping your front foot's toes on the line until you get to the next corner.*

- *Then move backward until your rear toes hit the rear line.*

- *Then move back in the other direction until you get to the last corner, finally moving back up the line to your starting position.*

- *As before, you'll do this a few times looking down at your feet to see you're stepping on the line each time, but as you get more proficient, you'll want to try completing the rectangle and getting back to your starting point, not by looking down, but simply by having good consistency, muscle memory, and sense of your body's position.*

Maintaining a good sense of your body's position in this way can help you avoid making a critical movement mistake and trapping yourself in a corner of the ring in a real match.

Intermediate Movement and Footwork Concepts

The basic mechanics of proper footwork can be understood and well-drilled in a relatively short period of time. I understand you probably already know all these basics. However, proper footwork remains an extremely difficult aspect of boxing because understanding and executing the basic mechanics in a highly controlled drill is so much different from doing it in a live sparring or boxing match. There's so much more to good footwork than just the basic mechanics. In the following section, we'll cover more of the intermediate details, common mistakes, and ways to improve your footwork beyond just mastering the basic mechanics.

Determining Range

The most important part of footwork is in controlling the range between yourself and your opponent. "Controlling the range" typically means maximizing the amount of time that you're in your own comfortable, ideal range for landing punches, and minimizing the same for your opponent. This is most starkly apparent if your opponent has a significantly different reach from you or a significantly different style in terms of where they most prefer to fight. The first thing you need to know is your range and your opponent's range, which is why many boxing matches begin with a sort of "feeling out" process where each fighter is throwing basic jabs more or less mainly to get a feel for exactly how far away their opponent needs to be for them to land a good punch.

Having a good feel for your own range before you get into a boxing match makes this process much easier and faster. The most obvious way to do this is simply by paying conscious attention to how close you like to stand to the heavy bag or a training partner holding mitts for you. The more subtle approach to really maximize your improvement in finding your range is to practice it while shadow boxing, make a conscious effort to visualize a live opponent in front of you, and practice your basic footwork. Having an actual live partner to practice footwork with can be even better.

Moving Away from the Opponent's Power Hand

The second big intermediate concept to always keep in mind is to try to always be moving away from the opponent's power hand, and simultaneously, try to move your own power hand toward the opponent. If you and the opponent are both orthodox or southpaw fighters, this generally means you are circling each other in the same direction. Much of the fight, then, is in a more or less neutral position in terms of lateral movement, with the main goal of footwork simply being to maintain your ideal punching range while avoiding the opponent's punching range. So, how can you do this?

For orthodox vs. orthodox: Step to your left, outside of their power right hand. Keep moving laterally rather than straight back. For orthodox vs. southpaw: Step to your right, away from their power left hand. Use small, sharp steps and avoid crossing your feet. Pivot off your lead foot to quickly change direction if needed. Maintaining distance is another way to avoid your opponent's power hand.

Stay just outside of the opponent's power punching range by using your footwork to maintain a safe distance, you can do this by stepping back or moving laterally just outside of their range. Use your jab to maintain distance and disrupt their rhythm when they try to close in. Stay aware of your positioning in the ring and use the ropes as boundaries to gauge how far back you can move.

Cutting Off the Ring

The final aim of superior footwork is generally referred to as "cutting off the ring," or, in the equal and opposite sense, preventing your opponent from being able to cut off the ring for you. In the great majority of fights, one fighter will generally want to be fighting at a closer range than the other, partly because of their reach relative to their opponent's, and partly because of their preferred fighting style. Some of the most violent and explosive matches happen when two fighters basically want to fight at the same range and are also equally matched in most other respects. They simply both agree upon a preferred range and just exchange punches from there until one or the other gets tagged or winded and has to back off to recover for an instant. The majority of matches, however, largely consist of each fighter in a constant struggle to use footwork to get out of the opponent's preferred range and into their own.

What this often looks like in practice is the fighter, who prefers to fight at the closer range, moves forward more often while the fighter, who prefers to fight at the longer range, circles away at the same speed, maintaining their own preferred range and comfortably throwing punches as the other fighter chases them. In order for the shorter ranged fighter to ever get to their own preferred range, they have to cut off the ring. Cutting off the ring, therefore, means stepping into the path that the other fighter wants to take to circle away - trying to trap them against the ropes of the ring, ideally in a corner.

Footwork Mistake #1: Not Practicing Visualization

I first had this epiphany when I was watching another fighter at my gym having their first professional match with our coach. The fighter was in fantastic shape, had excellent technique, was throwing with great speed and power, but was missing at least 80% of his punches. Lots of times he wasn't even close, he was just winging combinations from out of range and apparently seemed to be hoping his opponent would just walk into them. I asked our coach what he was doing, and the coach said, "He never visualizes when he practices his combinations, he only concentrates on his technique, speed, and power but not actually hitting his opponent." And sure enough, looking down at his feet told the tale; he would plant his feet out of range of the opponent, throw a wicked looking combination, miss, then reset and try again, but the opponent just moved back and watched the next combination miss, too.

In boxing, visualizing an opponent is crucial for maintaining effective footwork. Visualization is a mental training technique where a boxer mentally rehearses their movements, strategies, and desired outcomes before a fight. It involves imagining themselves executing perfect punches, defensive maneuvers, and tactics in the ring. Without this mental imagery, a boxer may move without direction or purpose, leading to aimless and inefficient footwork. Proper distance management becomes challenging without an opponent to gauge spacing, resulting in a boxer being too close or too far.

The key to avoiding this mistake is visualizing the opponent:

- *Where they are standing.*
- *Exactly how close you need to be to hit them.*
- *How to keep moving to follow them and keep them in range as they retreat or circle out.*

If you have a practice partner to work on footwork with, that's even better:

- *Take turns being the aggressor and defender.*

- *The aggressor tries to keep the defender in his ideal range while the defender tries to stay out of it, using proper footwork all the while.*

- *One thing to keep in mind though is that if the defender is actually the fighter with shorter reach, one of their best defensive tactics is actually to move forward right into clinching range and smother a longer-armed attacker.*

- *As the aggressor, you aren't necessarily always moving forward; you're trying to keep the ideal range, neither too far away to reach nor too close to throw properly.*

Footwork Mistake #2: Circling in the Wrong Direction

Beginner boxers often fall into the trap of circling in the wrong direction and opening themselves up to very effective power punches while putting themselves at a disadvantage when it comes to throwing effective power shots back. Occasionally switching up your movement to be less predictable is fine but be aware of the drawbacks so that you can anticipate and effectively defend yourself when you do.

If one fighter is orthodox and the other fighter southpaw, there is no laterally neutral position; you're both trying to circle into each other. The advantageous position in this situation is to have your front foot on the outside of theirs. When that happens, the opponent will be along your center line, but you will be outside of theirs. Any punches from their forward hand will be easier to see coming meaning you can easily parry or slip, and any punches from their rear hand will be coming from farther away, necessitating they turn their whole body that much more to even reach you.

At the same time, your forward hand will be able to throw much more effective lead hooks that will be harder to see coming, and straight punches from your power hand will be perfectly lined up to go straight "down the pipe" into the opponent. Therefore, effective lateral footwork is a huge part of fighting as or against a southpaw fighter. The fact that southpaw fighters generally get way more practice at training against orthodox fighters—a vital aspect of the game—is possibly the biggest reason that southpaw fighters tend to do better on average.

If a boxer circles towards their opponent's dominant hand (usually the rear hand), they move into the path of the most powerful punches, increasing the risk of getting hit by a strong hook or cross. For an orthodox vs orthodox bout, circling in the wrong direction would be circling around them to your left or in a clockwise direction, try to get out of the habit of doing this.

Again, the best way to drill this instinct into you is with a partner, where you're practicing your footwork with a conscious effort, circling and stepping away from the opponent's power hand while moving your power hand toward the opponent. When there isn't a practice partner available, visualization is your best tool to maximize your efficiency in improvement.

Footwork Mistake #3: Over-Correcting

A common mistake to be aware of as you practice is that there is a temptation to over-correct in terms of lateral stepping and movement such that you wind up too square-on to your opponent; a common mistake we already talked about above. Remember that the goal of moving your power hand into the range of the opponent should not come at the cost of losing power and opening yourself to hard straight punches by turning too square-on. Boxing, like so many things in life, is all about finding the perfect balancing point between two equal and opposite extremes. Here's a fun way to work on avoiding this common problem when drilling with a partner:

- *As you're each moving around each other, either have a third person randomly call out 'freeze,' or set a timer for about 20 seconds.*

- *When 'freeze' is called or the timer beeps, both of you instantly freeze and stop moving, and check your alignment.*

- *If one of you is more square on than the other, the other gets to do a light, slow, straight 'pushing' punch to the center of the body and the too-square-on partner has to stand there frozen and take it, understanding that if they were properly aligned it would glance off much more harmlessly.*

Of course, this drill can also be used to check for and 'punish' similar mistakes, like ending up too perpendicular, leaning too far forward or backward, and so on.

Footwork Mistake #4: Not Utilizing the Ring to Your Advantage

The difficulty of cutting off the ring or avoiding having the ring cut off for both fighters is the same: you have to move as quickly as possible but without sacrificing technique, leaving yourself open, or burning too much energy and tiring yourself out more than the opponent.

There are many ways to not use the ring to your advantage, backing into the corner or ropes limits your movement, not cutting off the ring allows your opponent to take control, excessive movement without purpose makes you fatigue quicker, staying stationary or moving in predictable patterns makes it easier for an opponent to anticipate and land punches and finally not using the entire ring limits your options.

All of the above puts you at a great disadvantage, so begin by identifying any of the bad habits you are currently guilty of and make an effort to break those bad habits. The key here is to improve your ring awareness.

A drill to fix these errors can simply be shadowboxing for 3 mins at a time in a ring or in a similar sized area. Throw multiple combinations against an imaginary opponent and after 4 or 5 combos, check where you are in the ring and get yourself into a better position if necessary. As you improve, start thinking about your positioning after each combo to prevent having to correct your position. You can make it more challenging by sparring a partner while maintaining ring awareness. Finally, make the ring/training area smaller so you get used to using less space - this will encourage you to use all the space much more effectively as you have nowhere to run.

Footwork Mistake #5: Sticky Feet

"Sticky feet" refers to when your feet feel too planted, heavy, dragging on the mat, slow, not springy and smooth. This is a very common problem for beginners, but actually has a very simple solution: get yourself some proper boxing shoes. When you replace your regular running or training shoes with proper boxing shoes, it's like removing training weights. Running shoes are designed for running. The grips are designed to hold your feet solidly to the ground and keep your feet straight so you don't twist your ankle, and they are made with thick, shock-absorbing soles so you can run long distances or at high speeds without damaging your joints from the shock of impacting the solid ground.

Boxing shoes are designed for boxing, funnily enough. The grips on boxing shoes provide good front-to-back grip but are designed to make it much easier to pivot your feet which is an essential part of throwing proper punches, as we'll get to later. But even more importantly for your footwork, they have much thinner soles, so they don't absorb energy when you're pushing off to step and move. The last thing you want is your shoes absorbing all your energy when you're trying to move quickly or throw solid punches. You don't need your shoes to absorb high-impact shocks when you're boxing; the ring itself has some padding already, and you're not killing your knees with sprinting or long-distance running in a boxing match; you're taking little steps and your feet are never much more than an inch off the ground anyway.

Footwork Mistake #6: Heel Stepping

Heel stepping means landing on your heel first as you move forward or leaving your heel on the ground last as you move backward. This is the natural, energy-saving way to walk, so it's how most people generally move around in a non-combat situation by default. The trade-off is that it's slow and awkward and makes it much tougher to defend yourself and throw effective punches or keep up with your opponent. Of course, the first solution is to simply practice your basic stepping technique, but even when you can do proper stepping that always begins and ends with the balls of your feet in practice, you may revert to heel stepping at any time in a live sparring session as you become tired, panicky, or uncomfortable as an opponent attacks you.

The real solution to heel stepping, even when you're tired or uncomfortable, is to get it into your instinctual muscle memory and improve your conditioning to the point that you're never too tired to step properly. The old standby training technique to do this is to jump rope (see Chapter 3, mistake #2). Jump rope is the best way to target the exact muscles and movements you need when you properly step off of and onto the balls of your feet. Not only that, but it helps improve your agility, your body coordination, and, as you get better, it will even help you maximize moving efficiently. As you get better and faster at skipping rope, you will find you need to lift your feet off the ground less and less.

Of course, there are other ways to improve your cardiovascular conditioning and leg strength, but apart from shadow boxing, nothing comes close to skipping rope in terms of mimicking the exact movements and targeting the exact muscles you'll need for proper footwork. Running is a great exercise, but you do very little running or anything like it in a boxing match. Squats improve your leg and back strength, but you aren't doing three sets of 10 squats in a boxing match—you're doing hundreds or thousands of little hops and steps. That's what you need your legs to be able to do, first and foremost.

Footwork Mistake #7: Getting Sloppy

Another common error that often comes from lack of conditioning is gradually losing technique and getting sloppy as you get tired, and generally the first thing that tends to go as people get sloppy is their footwork technique. The obvious solution is to just improve conditioning, but not only is that obvious, but there's also a limit. No matter what kind of condition you're in, unless your opponent is kind enough to get knocked out early, you're going to want to use all of your energy to try to win the fight. If you got to the end of the bout without feeling tired, that's more a sign that you could have fought harder and done more to win than that your conditioning is somehow perfect and superhuman.

Therefore, ideal boxing isn't about having such awesome conditioning that you can go full tilt with perfect technique for the entire duration of the bout because that's literally impossible; it's much more about having proper technique when needed and resting and being more energy efficient when you can get away with it. One of the main causes of getting sloppy when it matters is wearing yourself out unnecessarily by being too tense and inefficient with your energy usage.

So, for all of the advice on perfect movement technique, keeping your hands up, and so on, remember that it's necessary when, and only when, you're actually in range of your opponent. Much of the time spent in the ring with the opponent will be spent out of range of their punches. Having your hands up and moving with perfect technique when neither of you can reach the other with a punch is burning energy unnecessarily.

When you're circling away from the opponent out of their range or approaching them after the ref broke you up from a clinch, you can relax, have your hands a bit lower, take a more normal walking step, and only assume your proper stance and technique when you're in close enough range for it to matter. And even when you are in range of the opponent, don't be overly tense with your whole upper body.

Certain parts of your body need to be tense at certain times, like when you are throwing a punch or receiving a punch or taking a step, but keep the other parts of your body as loose and relaxed as possible. This will not only conserve your energy, but also improve your speed and reflexes. Keeping your whole body tense at all times because you're expecting that it makes you stronger and faster is like thinking that you're stronger and faster while carrying 20 pounds of groceries.

There isn't exactly a simple drill that's a quick or easy fix to this problem; it's largely a matter of putting in the time for sparring to get more comfortable with understanding safe distance so you know when you can relax a bit and how. Being consciously aware of this while you're sparring can help you improve more quickly.

Footwork Mistake #8: Straight, Predictable Movement

The final common errors to look out for are moving too straight, especially backward and forward, and being too predictable. This is something even experienced boxers do from time to time, and it typically happens for a few very understandable reasons.

The first big cause, especially of moving straight backward, is when a boxer gets hurt, stunned, or flustered. Particularly with beginner boxers that aren't used to having someone repeatedly punch them in the face (perfectly understandable!), your body's natural instinct is to move away from the threat as directly and rapidly as possible, and that generally means moving straight backward with your hands rigidly out in front, between your face and opponent. This instinctual defensive movement is exactly what an experienced boxer can capitalize on to finish the job, as they can accurately predict where your head is going to be and easily land a strong hooking punch to the chin while your hands are stiffly out in front of you.

The other common error is rushing straight forward into your opponent, which is another mistake that even experienced boxers can make, often when they think they've hurt the opponent. The opponent starts backing away quickly, and you want to keep in range to deliver the finishing punches before the opponent recovers. Then, pop! The opponent threw a straight counter down the pipe, and you rushed right into it.

The solution in both cases is to avoid straightforward or back movement. Instead, you want to move diagonally toward or away from your opponent so that your head is not in the same line at the end of your step as at the beginning, making it a harder target to predict and hit. If you're the one that's hurt and you want to back away from the opponent, always circle away, moving diagonally away from their power hand to mitigate some of its power, even if they do manage to hit you. And of course, keep your wits about you and your hands in the proper defensive position.

If you think you've hurt your opponent and you see them backing away quickly after you've landed a solid shot, you want to close back in, going for the finish. You should move diagonally, to cut off the ring and their possible escape path while avoiding any incoming counter punch that could put you down instead.

The best solution I've ever found to the very common problem of straight backward or forward movement is to practice it with a partner in a safe, low-impact, but still realistic way.

- *For the defensive part, have a practice partner throw very light punch combinations at you while you defend properly.*

- *For offense, do set drills with a partner where you will pretend to land a solid shot, your partner will back off like they're hurt, and you'll diagonally step to close down or maintain your effective punching range while avoiding an incoming counterpunch.*

The best time to do these kinds of exercises so that you will be able to do them correctly by instinct in a real match is to do them when you're already exhausted. You need to be able to keep your wits about you even when you're tired, hurt, or stunned, and you're panicking or looking for any way out, so practicing while already exhausted, but safely with low impact, is key.

5. Your Weak Punches

Boxing is all about effective punching, but punching effectively in live sparring or a real match can be one of the most difficult things for new boxers to master. Throwing a good punch seems simple enough in theory, but actually doing it in the heat of the moment against experienced opponents is another matter. Most beginners struggle with this most fundamental aspect of boxing, so we're going to tackle your punching and overall offense in this section. We'll break it down into three main sections. The first section will review the basic technical aspects of throwing a punch properly. The second section will add some more intermediate to advanced concepts for how to train and use punches effectively against a real opponent once you have the basic techniques down. The third section will go over common mistakes and give general tips for correcting them.

The Basics of Punching

In this section, we'll first talk about the basic mechanical techniques for each of the six main types of punches in boxing: jab, straight cross, lead hook, rear hook, lead uppercut, and rear uppercut. For future reference, when boxing coaches are calling out numbers for combinations, like the classic "one-two," they're referring to those punches in that order, so a jab is one, the straight cross is two, and so on. For each of these punching techniques, there are some individual variations that can be situationally effective. For example, a variation on the straight cross is the overhand punch, sometimes called a 'haymaker' when thrown wide, looping, and sloppy; or the shovel hook, which is sort of halfway between a hook and uppercut.

The jab: the basic front-hand punch, straight toward the opponent. Keep your elbow tight and down and concentrate on throwing it quickly with a 'snap'. It's mostly a set-up punch for your offense, or an opportunistic punch to disrupt your opponent's offense. The bullet points below show you how to throw a jab, remember to start in your boxing stance holding your guard.

- *You do not need to load up the jab because it's not meant to land with extreme power. A good stiff jab to get someone's attention is efficient.*

- *Do not telegraph your jab. This means to not give away that you are about to throw a jab as your opponent could easily defend and counter it.*

- *With your lead hand in front, extend your punch straight out. Move only your front arm and nothing else.*

- *The extension should be quick and relaxed. Imagine your hand being like a whip and just shooting forward with little consequence.*

- *As your hand extends out, rotate your arm right before the punch lands, so the palm section of your hand is facing down. The entire arm, including the shoulder, elbow, wrist, and fist, will rotate.*

- *Lift your shoulder slightly for better reach and to protect your chin more.*

- *Tighten your fist right at the moment of impact for a better snap. As your fist tightens, your entire body contracts for explosiveness for a quick second.*

- *Your arm should be completely extended out and rotated at the end of your jab.*

- *Avoid tensing up before the punch lands. Otherwise, you are wasting extra energy.*

- *Once the jab lands, pull your hand straight back to its original position.*

The straight cross: the basic rear hand punch, also straight toward your opponent. Throw with your whole body, starting at the feet, and turn into the punch from your toes, ankles, knees, hips, and shoulders. This is a power punch that works well when set up by the jab or as a counter punch. A variation on this punch is throwing it 'overhand,' often as you are ducking forward, which can create a deceptive angle of attack.

- *Get into a proper stance with your non-dominant side at the forward lead. For this example, it will be your left side.*

- *Rotate your right hip forward while pivoting on your right foot. Your heel should come off the ground.*

- *Shift your weight forward and extend your right arm to punch.*

- *As you extend, rotate your arm and hand, so your palm is facing downward.*

- *Tighten your fist as you make an impact.*

- *After landing the punch, quickly snap back your hand to cover your face.*

The lead hook: A hook thrown with your front hand, this punch can be used at long range as a set-up punch that comes from a different angle than a jab, or at range as part of a hard combination. Throw to the body as well for very punishing liver shots.

- *Get into your desired boxing stance based on the principles we discussed earlier.*

- *Maintain proper defense with good hand placement and eye contact.*

- *Make sure you close the distance with your opponent. The hook is a short-range punch.*

- *There will be some loading involved. This is why you really have to wait for the right opening and not just throw the punch carelessly.*

- *When you have an opening, whether the body or head, pull back your arm quickly and then release the punch.*

- *Load up your hook by slightly twisting your body towards your lead hand.*

- *Release the punch. As you throw the hook, pivot your feet into the hook to keep your momentum moving forward. Push through with the ball of your feet.*

- *Rotate your arm as you are moving, so the palm section is facing down.*

- *Tighten your fist right before impact.*

- *After the hook lands, quickly bring your hand back to its original position to keep your defense.*

The rear hook: a hook thrown from your backhand, this punch is most common as a finishing punch in a combination, but also useful to punish an opponent standing too perpendicular to you. Same concept as lead hook, just throw with the dominant hand.

- *Begin in your boxing stance.*

- *Ensure you are in close proximity to your target.*

- *Engage your core and take your right hand slightly away from your face.*

- *Pivot on your right foot and throw your punch toward the target in an arc.*

- *Keep your arm at a 90-degree angle throughout the punch. Your elbow should be in line with your fist and shoulder. At the moment of impact, your palm can face you or downwards, depending on preference and target.*

- *After making contact, follow through slightly to ensure the punch has maximum impact, but avoid overextending.*

- *Quickly bring your hand back to guard your face to avoid counterpunches.*

The lead uppercut: Thrown in an upward direction with your lead hand, this is a great punch to punish opponents that lean in and duck down predictably and can also be used to punish the body or even as a long-range set-up punch that comes from a deceptive angle.

- *Start in your stance.*

- *Begin the uppercut by bending your knees, slightly dropping your body down.*

- *Keep your hips down and rotate your hips and shoulders toward your lead side - left for orthodox.*

- *After rotating your body slightly either to your lead side, slightly drop your lead hand from your face and punch up towards the target, use your legs to drive your body upward. Pivot your feet into the direction of the punch.*

- *Keep your elbows bent and close to your body. The punch should travel in a tight arc, not a wide swing (don't over-exaggerate it). Keep your palms facing your body.*

- *Transfer your weight from your back foot to your front foot. After the punch lands, pull your hand straight back to your chin. Remember, the punch is just supposed to pop their head up quickly.*

The rear uppercut: A great finishing punch to pierce a tight closed guard after setting it up with some powerful hooks. Same as a lead uppercut, just the opposite hand.

- *Follow the instructions for the lead uppercut, just use the opposite side.*

Common Technical Errors

Out of all the techniques, it is probably easiest for boxers to identify their poor punching technique because landing a punch improperly feels awkward and can be quite painful. However, they often struggle to find the exact flaw as most punching mistakes come from a weak stance or poor footwork, so be mindful of this before trying to correct your punches.

However, there are still many punching mistakes that diminish the power, accuracy, and effectiveness of their strikes. These errors, such as dropping the hands, telegraphing punches, or overextending, not only reduce the impact of the punches but also leave a fighter vulnerable to counterattacks. Understanding and correcting these mistakes is essential for improving overall performance in the ring and maintaining a strong defensive posture.

Jab Mistakes

- Slightly moving the punching arm down before throwing the jab - Dropping your arm before jabbing signals your intention to your opponent, giving them a clear visual cue to anticipate and prepare for the punch.

    - *Don't move your arm down, throw the jab straight out with the power of your rotating body.*

    - *Record yourself practicing the jab (either with a partner or bag) to see if this is a mistake you're making.*

- Flaring your elbow as you throw the punch - Punches should follow the most direct path to the target. Flaring the elbow adds an unnecessary arc to the punch, slowing it down and reducing its overall efficiency.

    - *Practice getting the motion of twisting your wrist without flaring out your elbow.*

    - *Although you twist your wrist, do not bend it at any time. Your hand should be extended in a straight line.*

- Over-rotating and extending - This can cause you to lose your balance, making it difficult to quickly recover and defend against counterattacks. It also uses more energy than necessary.
    - *Try to master at least two speeds of jab: one that is a more powerful, stiffer jab that incorporates your whole body and has the potential to stun anyone it catches clean, and a quicker jab that doesn't involve foot and leg rotation but begins at the hips so it's less telegraphed and slightly snappier.*
- Raising your chin and/or dropping your non-punching hand - Here you are just asking to take a clean punch to your face.
    - *Make sure your non-punching hand is always raised to keep the guard strong.*
- Laziness/ taking shortcuts - A lazy jab lacks the speed, precision, and snap required to be effective.
    - *After landing your jab, bring your hand back and reset to your neutral stance as quickly as possible.*
    - *Punch through your target.*

- Forgetting about the jab - Neglecting it diminishes your overall punching volume and limits your ability to apply consistent pressure on your opponent.
    - *Don't use the jab as just an opening move or to feel out the range; the jab can be used as an offensive, defensive, and counter move.*

Straight Cross Mistakes

- Excessive head movement (moving your head in the same direction as the punch) - This can throw you off balance and leave you vulnerable to counterattacks.

    - *Record yourself practicing the cross (either with a partner or bag) to see if this is a mistake you're making and make a conscious effort to stop it.*

- Opening your elbow before throwing the punch - This shows your intention and makes it easier for your opponent to react to your cross.

    - *You can practice throwing this punch near a wall to keep your elbow from flaring out.*

- Only using one shoulder - This will reduce the power you generate and limit your defensive capabilities.

    - *You need to use both shoulders to effectively throw a straight cross, therefore ensure you engage both shoulders while throwing the cross. Your lead shoulder should rotate back and your rear shoulder should rotate forward.*

- Underrotating your heel - This limits this rotation, resulting in a weaker punch because you can't utilize the full kinetic chain effectively.
    - *Your heel should be raised off the ground and your toes rotated inward.*

Lead Hook Mistakes

- Not loading your hook - This limits your range of motion and reduces power generation.
  - *The 'loaded' position for a power lead hook looks similar to the end of a straight cross, so practice following a straight cross with a power lead hook, called the "two-three" combination, this will help you load up the hook properly and is a great power combination you can use.*

- Only focusing on the head - Not only are you being predictable but you are missing golden opportunities to drop your opponent with a body shot.
  - *Hooks are effective as both body and head shots and are equally effective at very close or medium range.*
  - *When you practice your hooks, practice them at all ranges to both body and head height.*

- Bending your wrist - You are risking injury and your punch will lack power.

- *You'll get more power by keeping your hand in line with your wrist rather than bending it, plus you'll avoid breaking your wrist on impact.*

- Dropping the rear hand while throwing the punch - Opening yourself for counterattacks.

Rear Hook Mistakes

- Not twisting all the way around - This can throw off your center of gravity, making you more vulnerable to counterattacks and reducing your ability to recover quickly after the punch.

    - *If you do not finish a rear hook with your shoulders twisted all the way around until your rear punching hand's shoulder is pointed in line to the opponent, your hook will look and feel terrible and be a totally ineffective pure "arm punch". Aim for your forearm to point straight at your opponent at the end of the hook.*

- Not utilizing your stance - You can't transfer your body's full power into the punch, resulting in a weaker strike.

    - *One unique aspect of the rear hook is that it can come with even more power when you open your stance slightly and finish the punch with your stance being slightly more square on to your opponent than would otherwise be normal or ideal.*

- *Incorporating rear hooks into combinations with lateral or diagonal movement can be highly effective.*

- Not resetting your foot position relative to your opponent - You can easily be knocked off balance in this position.

  - *Practice throwing rear hooks when shadowboxing or with a partner and build a habit of resetting your foot potion immediately after you land the punch.*

- Throwing haymakers - If you are relying on wildly hitting and hoping to win your fights, consider an alternative.

  - *Generally, it looks sloppy, is easy to block or avoid, and hits with much less power than it looks like it has.*

  - *Throwing haymakers is generally an ineffective, instinctual, flailing technique used by non-boxers that are either panicking or in a rage.*

Uppercut Mistakes

- Moving your body incorrectly.

    - *Beginners feel inclined to move their whole body from a downward to upward motion when they throw uppercuts, like a character in Street Fighter or Mortal Kombat, but in fact, the body motions for throwing a proper uppercut are very similar to throwing the other punches.*

    - *Almost all of your body movement is twisting along the horizontal plane, not moving vertically at all.*

    - *At the very most, you may dip your shoulder a little bit at the beginning of throwing an uppercut and then raise it again on the follow-through, but that's as far as your body should move vertically.*

    - *You do not crouch down or bend over and then lift your whole body up to throw a decent uppercut.*

- Too slow - You leave lots of opportunity for a counter.

- Punching too high or too low - This can leave you vulnerable and you will lack power.

Intermediate Attacking Concepts

Once you have the basic techniques down in terms of your shadow boxing, hitting the heavy bag, and mitt work, you need to be able to master some intermediate concepts in order to use your punches effectively in any kind of live sparring or real match situation. Below we'll go over some of the most useful intermediate-level concepts that new boxers often run into difficulties until they master them.

Effective Use of the Jab

The jab is a very important and even versatile punch that is often underestimated or underappreciated by new boxers and casual fans of boxing even though you'll often hear boxing commentators and analysts talking about it. The main uses of the jab are to find your range, control the distance, set up combinations, and disrupt the opponent's offense. Because the jab is the quickest, safest, and least energy-expending punch to throw, it is usually the best choice for accomplishing each of those objectives. It's not flashy or devastating or likely to get you any one-punch knockouts, but it's a critical part of the game, and using it poorly or not often enough is a very common beginner mistake.

Jabbing to find range is generally done at the beginning of the match and should only take a few moments; you make note of where your feet are relative to the opponent as you throw your jab and fix it in your unconscious memory while finding the right range.

Jabbing to control the distance has two aspects; if you are the fighter with the longer range, you throw out heavy, stiff jabs immediately when the opponent steps closer into their range and use that punch as cover to circle out and away, maintaining your own ideal range. If you are the fighter that wants to close the distance, you can throw out lighter, faster, distracting jabs as you step in, which can discourage the opponent from punching you at the same time and cover your movement closer. Sure, the opponent can still step away, but if the whole fight is you throwing punches as you move toward your opponent while they are just stepping away, you're looking way better on any judge's scorecard.

Jabbing to set up combinations has two aspects as well. The first is to throw out a jab in order to see how your opponent responds to it; do they duck or slip? In which direction? Do they block or parry? With which hand? After you note their reaction, you can predict their defense and then add a second punch to get around that defense. The second use of the jab is that it naturally loads up your power hand as you throw it, which gets your power hand in position to throw with power immediately afterward. As you practice punching combinations, you'll notice that you can harness the effect of using jabs and left-right combinations in general to load up second, third, and fourth punches in your combinations and throw them naturally with more power than if you had just thrown them from your neutral stance as a first punch.

Jabbing to disrupt the opponent's offense is another great use of the jab as a defensive or counter-offensive technique. As you get more comfortable in sparring, you'll gain a better ability to anticipate opponents. Once you've mastered your own technique basics, you can devote more of your concentration to paying attention to your opponent and their tendencies and habits. You'll be able to pick up on that and see when they want to throw a punch. And once you do that, you can interrupt their punch by throwing out a faster jab of your own first, disrupting their offense and stopping their combination cold. The best time to land a punch is when the opponent is throwing one of their own, and a good stiff jab that lands cleanly can stun or even knock down an opponent that doesn't see it coming because they're concentrating on throwing their own punch at the same time.

Offensive Variety

Another important aspect of the offensive game is to make it harder on your opponent by being somewhat unpredictable. Don't throw out the same punches every time or even more than twice in a row, or your opponent will very quickly get in your head, anticipate you, and not just nullify your attacks, but counter you with effective offense of their own. Boxing, in some ways, is like a game of rock-paper-scissors, where each technique can counter another, so using the right technique at the right time is critical. If you're throwing out 'rock' every time you play rock-paper-scissors, it won't be too long before your opponent just throws out paper every time and you never win.

Therefore, it's important to mix up your offense with a good variety of techniques. Throw body shots as often as you go to the head of your opponent, so they don't know where to defend. Throw both straight shots and hooks and mix in uppercuts if the opponent is bending at the waist. When you throw, throw in combinations and incorporate your footwork and upper body movement to mix up the angle and range of your combinations. You should master throwing your punches with perfect technique from your neutral stance first, but once you have done that, you can begin working on throwing good punches even while stepping and moving, and while leaning your body left or right to avoid incoming punches and throw simultaneous counter attacks from unexpected angles.

Finally, particularly if your opponent is very slick about leaning and using rapid head movements to make you miss, double or triple up on your same hand when throwing combinations rather than always going left-right-left-right. Going left-left-left instead can be faster and leave your opponent with no room left to lean, forcing them way off balance. Sure, the second or third left will have basically no power because you've had no chance to reload your punch fully, but it will still be unpleasant for your opponent to get bopped in the face, and once they're way off balance trying to avoid your second or third shots, then you can come in with a power right they won't see coming or have no room left to avoid anyway.

Effective Counter Punching and Feints

Many of the greatest boxers of all time use counter-punching as the bread and butter of their game plan. Being an effective counter-puncher requires being very comfortable and confident in the ring and having mastered the basics of your own techniques to the point that you can concentrate all your attention on the opponent and anticipate what they're going to do. As I've already said many times, the best time to hit your opponent is when they're trying to hit you. Once your opponent has at least one hand away from their head and body, that's one less hand you have to avoid to land your own punch cleanly. Not only that, but your opponent will have planted their feet to throw their punch with any kind of power, and that will make your own punch land more solidly. Considering their mind is on their offense, if your own punch lands at that time, it will be more surprising to them, and they'll react more poorly to absorb it.

  Of course, effective counterpunching is far more easily said than done. And how can you avoid being the victim of effective counterpunching yourself? Well, as said above, varying your offense is a great start. Another important tool in the box is to use feints effectively. If you find yourself against a very slick opponent that is very hard to hit and always seems ready to counter, feints are the best answer. Every time you feint a punch and your opponent moves to defend it, in all likelihood you made them move more than you did. A feint can be just a quick jerk of your shoulders, a twist of your hips, a flick of a hand, and if you made them take a step back, slip, lean, or parry thin air, they probably burned more energy than you did. Eventually, they're going to get tired of overreacting to your feints, and that's going to slow them down and make them lazier when it comes to reacting to your real punches. And of course, you can use feints like a jab, see how the opponent reacts, anticipate, and then throw the next punch accordingly.

Fighting Effectively in Close

If you have a shorter reach than your opponent, or compared to most opponents, you may find your best opportunities while fighting very close to the opponent. There are two difficulties to doing so, however. The first is that your opponent will most likely be constantly circling away to avoid you getting into your comfort zone, so you'll have to have the footwork and jab game to cut off the ring from your opponent and get in close without eating heavy punches that stun you. The second is that if you do manage to get in close, any experienced opponent is going to do everything they can to "tie you up" in a 'clinch.' A clinch happens when one or both boxers wrap up the others' arms in their own so that neither fighter can throw any punches, at which point, the referee will stop the fight and separate the fighters safely before restarting the fight. If you're the fighter that wants to be in close, you just get sent back to square one.

Solving the first problem is a matter of having better footwork and a good jab. Solving the second problem requires working on your close-in fighting to throw good punches without getting tied up. The key to avoiding being tied up is to understand the three ways in which you can get tied up, the specific ways to avoid each of them, and to keep your hands and arms free to throw punches:

1. **Headlock**. With this tie-up technique, the opponent will wrap an arm around your head and pull it down and to the side, pulling you off balance, perhaps turning their back so you cannot throw a legal shot. The key to avoiding a headlock is to keep your head down, pressing your forehead into their head or chest, and if you feel their arm coming around behind your head, duck your head a bit more, shrug your shoulders, and let their arm slide off you. Push against their chest with both hands to create a bit of space and prevent them from turning their back and throw a punch or two before they recover their guard.

2. **Overhook**. With this tie-up technique, the opponent will try to trap your arms against their side by wrapping their arms over the top of yours. If they manage to do so, it will take a ton of your energy to pull your arms out because they'll be squeezing your arms and your boxing gloves will get stuck as you try to extricate yourself. If this happens, most boxers will just save their energy and wait for the ref to break it up. To avoid it happening, keep your gloves in the middle of their body so that they cannot get their arms around yours, and keep your elbows tight to your body to protect from punches to your side. Use your head and shoulders to push off to create a bit of distance to throw punches rather than pushing with your hands so that your hands will not slip past their body and allow them to wrap you up.

3. **Underhook**. With this tie-up technique, they are pushing their hands under your armpits and around your body, hugging you close to them so there's no distance for you to throw a punch with any power. To avoid this from happening, keep your elbows extra tight to your body so there's no room for your opponent to slide their gloves through, and keep your hips back away from their hips so they cannot pull you in close.

You can practice these techniques with a heavy bag by putting your forehead and shoulder right against the heavy bag, pulling your hips back a bit, and practice unleashing with power from point-blank range while keeping your elbows tight to your body at all times to avoid leaving any opening for your opponent to tie you up in any way.

Precision Beats Power, Timing Beats Speed

This is a common saying in the combat sports world, made famous by Conor McGregor but known by generations of boxers and other combat sports athletes. The points it makes are general truisms when it comes to striking effectiveness; landing your shots precisely on target does more damage than missing or glancing more powerful shots and timing your strikes to land perfectly is more effective than trying to beat an opponent with raw speed alone. But it's easier said than done, right? It's fairly straightforward to train power and speed; just practice hitting things harder and punching faster, but how do you train precision and timing? Well, in fact there are some things you can do to improve those aspects of your game too, and as the expression implies, you should be spending at least as much total training time on your precision and timing as you do on improving your power and speed.

The most obvious way to work on precision and timing is with a training partner holding mitts for you, giving you moving targets and forcing you to anticipate, accurately aim, and time your punches to land cleanly. When you're not working with a training partner, working a speed bag can improve your timing, and another common drill is to shadow box with a tennis ball and practice dropping it and catching it between punches, or even bouncing it off the ground.

The movie *Rocky III* features an amusing sequence with Duke trying to get Rocky to do this drill effectively, but it's actually a real thing. Practicing bouncing and catching a tennis ball between punches while moving around and shadow boxing can improve your overall body coordination, accuracy, and timing. These drills, along with the overall mindset of focusing on your precision and timing, can help you focus on your opponent during a match, anticipate their timing, look for and even create opportunities to land precise, well-timed strikes, and capitalize on them to win the match.

Common Punching Errors

The most common punching errors usually stem from incorrect stance or poor footwork, which is why we covered those aspects of the game first. But assuming that your stance and footwork have already been corrected and improved, here are a few other common errors specifically just to do with throwing punches:

- Leaving your hands hanging out there and being lazy about resetting to your neutral stance after each punch. Unless you are specifically doing a same-hand combination, always bring your punching hand back to its proper defensive and loaded position as quickly as possible. Whatever you do, don't drop it down to your side or hip first, or you will surely get countered and tagged cleanly.

- Dropping, pulling, or otherwise forgetting about the non-punching hand. The hand that is not punching has to stay up by your face protecting your jaw from any counter or simultaneous punch, and your elbow has to be down right to your ribs and body protecting your liver or pancreas as much as possible. Also, if you're in the habit of moving your non-punching hand just before or as you're throwing, that's a tell that your opponent can take advantage of to predict your punch, avoid it, and counter you.

- Throwing from out of range. This is more a footwork issue, but always make sure you move your feet into range before or while you are throwing so that your punches can reach your opponent, otherwise you're just wasting energy.

- Holding your breath while punching. This is a very common beginner issue; humans have a natural tendency to hold our breath while exerting maximum force, but holding your breath while punching will leave you out of breath and exhausted in minutes if not seconds. Get into the habit of exhaling on every punch to make sure you aren't doing this.

- Raising and exposing your chin while punching. Make sure you keep your chin down and tucked at all times to avoid being knocked out with a counter punch.

- Lifting the hips while turning into punches. This is another common technique mistake that saps your power a bit with unnecessary vertical movement and also throws off your balance a bit making it easier to knock you over with a counter punch.

- No head movement. Keep your head moving, in and out and left and right, before and after you throw to make your punches less predictable and make yourself harder to hit with counters.

- Losing track of your opponent. Newer boxers often lose sight and lose track of their opponent and what their opponent is doing while they are punching, especially if they're throwing a complex combination; try to keep your eyes, focus, and attention on your opponent at all times.

How to Fix Common Punching Errors

- The best way to work on your punches is to begin with the most basic techniques, recording yourself throwing them to catch your mistakes, and correcting them before they become bad habits. Perhaps watch through them with a coach or experienced boxer so they can point out the flaws, or even compare your technique to those of professional fighters.

- Also, if something *feels* bad, it probably *is* bad. A properly thrown punch feels great to throw. You feel fast, you feel powerful, you feel like you could put your hand right through a brick wall (don't actually try to put your hand through a brick wall no matter how tempting it may be).

- If you don't feel right, you aren't getting it right, so break your movement down into each tiny detail to spot the flaws and correct them until it does feel right, then try to replicate it smoothly and add speed and power with each repetition.

Once you have some of the basic movements of each technique down, work on training with a heavy bag and with a training partner holding mitts. That will help you get a feel for how to punch through a target with power, how to actually hit a moving target, and how to link punches in combinations without leaving yourself open. I have given you all the information you need to identify where you are going wrong with punching and how you can correct your errors to improve as a boxer. There will be more on advanced training techniques in Chapter 7.

6. Your Poor Defense

There's an old chestnut in boxing that the last thing you want to be known for as a fighter is your chin or your toughness. As Frankie said in *Million Dollar Baby*, "Show me a fighter who's nothing but heart, and I'll show you a man waiting for a beating." A good defense means you don't need to rely on your chin, your toughness, or your heart to survive a boxing match. To borrow from George Patton, good boxing isn't about being able to rely on your chin; it is about making the other guy rely on their chin, toughness, and heart to survive the match with you. So, if you find yourself getting tagged a lot in sparring, there are probably some very basic defensive errors you're making that, if fixed, could save you pain and effort in the ring. Of course, the ultimate example of the power of good defense is the ultimate defensive fighter, Floyd Mayweather Jr., who built a perfect 50-0 record on his ability to make opponents miss almost everything they threw at him.

There's a well-known principle that the best defense is a good offense, which is true in boxing to a certain extent, but it is equally true that the best offense is a good defense. You cannot have a good boxing game without having both. No matter how good your defensive movements and techniques are in boxing, if you cannot throw a good enough punch to make your opponent respect you; your opponent will simply tee off on you until something eventually lands clean, or you're forced to spend the whole fight running away and getting docked points for timidity, stalling, or refusing to engage, so a good offense is definitely necessary for a good defense. By the same token however, a good defense sets up your offense, tires and frustrates your opponent, and of course, allows you to fight longer and more confidently to give you more opportunities to use your offensive techniques.

Basic Defensive Techniques

The basic defensive techniques to master are blocking, parrying, slipping, ducking, rolling and clinching. Master these basic techniques and when to use them, and you will make yourself a much more frustrating opponent to face in the ring, as well as protect yourself from unnecessary pain.

- *Blocking is the act of repositioning your guard to block punches with your forearms or gloves. There are a few variations on hand positions, like the high guard, the cross guard, and so on, with their own pros and cons. Generally speaking, this is a last resort defense when you're not sure where the next punch is coming and should immediately be followed up by either a full disengagement or going for a clinch.*

- *Parrying is when you use your own hand to deflect an incoming punch. Generally, you want to deflect incoming jabs, and redirect the opponent's punch across their body so their hands get crossed, creating an opening for your own counterpunches. The three main types of parrying are the down parry, the side parry and the circle parry. Parrying power punches is risky as you need more strength to do that effectively, and if the opponent tricks you with a feint, doing a 'stronger' parry puts your own hand out of position and opens you up to their real punch.*

- *Slipping is when you turn your hips and shoulders together in order to move your head left or right to avoid a straight punch, often accompanied by a slight complementary lean as well. The key is to keep the movement as subtle as possible to make the punch barely miss; moving too much wastes energy and can throw you off balance, making resetting yourself to avoid the next punch in the combination too slow.*

- *Ducking tends to refer to bending at the waist and leaning forward to make the opponent miss high and/or long. As with slipping, you want to keep your movement as subtle as you can while still making the opponent miss, especially while leaning away. When it comes to ducking forward, you tend to need a much more dramatic movement; beware of uppercuts when doing this and when you are ducking down and coming back up, make sure you do it diagonally, in the direction away from their power hand to be safer. Don't forget to keep your eyes on your opponent at all times. Leaning back is usually best used against uppercuts and sometimes hooks, while ducking is strictly for hooks and power straight or overhand punches.*

- *Rolling, or shoulder rolling, is basically the same movement as slipping but with more emphasis on raising and using your shoulder to deflect and absorb some of the incoming punch. This is usually best used against straight punches.*

- *Clinching is when you move right into your opponent and tie up their arms with your own, either by wrapping up their arms in an overhook or pulling them close with an underhook, sometimes with one arm around their head to control their head and limit their movement as well. When this happens, the referee immediately steps in to break up the fighters, so you can get a chance to safely reposition yourself to a neutral position, which can save you when you are stunned or getting overwhelmed by combinations.*

Drills to Improve Your Defense

Once you've practiced the basic mechanics of these defensive techniques in front of a mirror, the most important thing is to work on them with a training partner. In fact, with some of them, especially parrying and clinching, it's practically impossible to even work on them at all without a training partner. However, there are many things you can do to improve your defensive game even on your own just in terms of improving your speed, reflexes, and defensive awareness and good habits. Below are 4 drills to aid your defensive ability.

Defense Drill #1 - Mirrored Shadowboxing

The first and easiest thing is to work on good defensive habits in front of a mirror while shadow boxing:

- While doing your standard shadow boxing workout, practicing your combinations and punching form in front of a mirror, focus on the reflection as if it's another boxer throwing counter punches back at you.

- Use this focus as a reminder to keep your non-punching hand up and move your head before and after and even during punches.

- Bring your punching hand back to its ready position quickly after each punch.

- This will take some getting used to, be patient and watch clips of mirrored shadowboxing if it helps.

Defense Drill #2 - Rope Slip and Duck

The second common training drill is to slip and duck under a rope:

- Begin by hanging up a rope, line, or even a stretched-out hand-wrap in a straight line at head height.

- Then, practice slipping and ducking under it from side to side while moving forward and backward. I recommend a round of slipping, a round of ducking and a round where you mix it up.

- As said above, the important thing with slipping is not to over-exaggerate the movement and throw yourself off balance and expend too much energy.

- When practicing with a hanging line like this, you can practice moving just enough to clear the rope with each slip.

- As you get a feel for just the right amount of movement, you can then add speed until you're moving fast enough to avoid any incoming punch.

Defense Drill #3 - Tennis Ball Reflex

- Another basic drill that improves your hand-eye coordination to particularly help with parrying is to simply throw a tennis ball against a wall and catch it or bounce it back against the wall, as quickly and as close to the wall as you can.

- Try to aim the ball so it will come back at your head and body, so you get used to watching something coming at you and moving your hand to intercept it before it gets there.

- As you improve, you can throw the ball with more speed to make it harder to intercept.

Defense Drill #4 - Heavy Bag Block and Clinch

A good drill to work on both your blocking and clinching on your own is to practice it while working a heavy bag:

- Normally while working a heavy bag, if you time your punches properly, it won't swing around wildly, and you'll get a feel for that as you get better.

- To practice your defense, you can intentionally get the bag swinging toward you, then lean into it, and let it hit your guard to stop it, then work it inside with your forehead right against the bag for a combination or two.

- Then, practice clinching it up; imagine it as an opponent with arms that you need to trap and wrap up.

- When you've stopped the bag, step back and start over, constantly visualizing a real opponent that's really swinging at you, charging into you when you're stunned, and you need to block a few heavy punches, lean into it, throw a few counters of your own, and tie it up.

When you've mastered the basic techniques, you can take your defensive game to the next level by using your strong defenses to bait out attacks you expect and then countering them effectively. A truly great defensive game is characterized by confidence, comfort, rhythm, and aggression. You aren't just defending and backing away from the opponent; you're leaning into them, making them miss, and then making them pay. You see everything coming and none of it bothers you; in fact, you already expected it, and you already knew how you were going to counter it. That's the kind of defense that wins fights.

Common Defensive Technical Mistakes

In boxing, mastering defense is just as crucial as developing powerful punches and slick footwork. However, even experienced fighters can fall into common defensive mistakes that leave them vulnerable to counterattacks and knockdowns. These mistakes are often a result of a poor stance or lazy footwork, however assuming that you have worked on those areas of your game and are still struggling to make great use of the defensive techniques just discussed, here we cover the common errors of the defensive techniques.

Blocking Mistakes

- Telegraphing the block - Making obvious movements to block punches can give your opponent cues about your intentions.

- Using only one hand to block - This can make you predictable and expose the unguarded side of your face and body. Utilize both hands for a balanced defense.

- Blocking too close to your face - Keeping your hands too close to your face can absorb the full impact of the punch, leading to potential injury.

- Blocking without moving - Relying solely on blocks without incorporating footwork and head movement makes you a stationary target. Use footwork to create angles and move away from the opponent's line of attack.

For a corrective drill, first identify the mistake you make, if you make all 4 that's not an issue. Next, get in front of a mirror and practice going from your regular stance to a high guard block and then a low guard block. Check where your hands are and see if your positioning is good. Then get into rounds of shadowboxing, visualize an opponent throwing punches at you and make an effort to correct your errors.

Remember to keep moving, use both hands, and don't make your next move obvious. As you feel like you can block without needing to think about it, practice blocking shots from a partner - make sure they are aware of your previous errors and ask them to stop when you do slip up. Eventually, you iron out these mistakes and begin to block properly.

Parrying Mistakes

The most common mistakes with parrying are parrying with the wrong hand in the wrong direction, or misjudging the timing of the parry, possibly because you got taken in by feints.

- Overcommitting - This means pushing your hand too far out when attempting to parry. This can leave you off-balance and open to follow-up punches.

- Parrying too early or too late - Parrying too early can expose you to follow-up punches, while parrying too late means you might still get hit.

- Parrying with the wrong hand - Using the wrong hand to parry can leave you exposed. Use the hand that is closest to the incoming punch to deflect it effectively.

- Telegraphing the parry - Making large, obvious movements to parry a punch can signal your intentions to your opponent. This can allow them to feint and exploit your reaction.

Yet again, the only way to overcome your mistakes is to practice the defensive technique with your focus on not making that mistake. Please keep this approach to every defensive technique. Remember, training 1-on-1 with a partner is the greatest way to overcome any flaws in your technique, you can easily get carried away when training alone and get back into your bad habits. Falling that, record yourself, take a few minutes between each time you practice to review yourself.

Slipping Mistakes

The common errors in slipping are in moving too much, burning too much energy and being unable to quickly return to neutral, by misjudging your opponent's timing and getting hit, or in being unable to effectively counter after slipping.

- Over-Slipping - Moving your head too far to the side when slipping can take you out of position, making it harder to counter and recover.

- Dropping hands - Lowering your hands while slipping can leave your face unprotected and expose you to follow-up punches.

- Neglecting footwork - Failing to move your feet when slipping can make you a stationary target, reducing the effectiveness of the slip.

- Inconsistent head movement - Slipping only occasionally or inconsistently can make your defensive rhythm predictable.

Ducking Mistakes

The common errors with ducking are moving too much or too little to avoid the incoming punches, or misjudging the type of punch the opponent is throwing and doing the wrong movement. For example, if you try to lean away from a power straight right, the opponent may have the reach to hit you anyway, and it can send you way off balance. Ducking into an uppercut is even worse. As with perfecting your slipping, the best thing to do is work with a partner:

- *Have your partner start with 30 reps of doing very slow and predictable punches for you to lean away from or duck under as appropriate with your hands down.*

- *Next, do 30 more with your hands up.*

- *Then 30 more while being less predictable, forcing you to pay attention to what is coming.*

- *Finally, 30 more punches with you integrating counters.*

Some of the best counter punches you can throw are a straight rear power punch after successfully leaning away from a hook or uppercut and coming with a power hook or uppercut after successfully ducking under an opponent's hook or straight power punch.

Rolling Mistakes

- Overcommitting - Moving your upper body too far off the centerline or bending excessively can throw you off balance and make it difficult to counter or recover.

- Not using legs and hips - Relying solely on your upper body for the rolling motion can lead to poor balance and ineffective defense.

- Leaning forward - Leaning too far forward when rolling can compromise your balance and make you vulnerable to uppercuts.

- *The best drill to perfect rolling is with a partner throwing very light straight punches down the line and you planting your feet in range and avoiding them, to the left and to the right, over and over again.*

- *Get a nice rhythm going at first, keep your hands down a bit at first, and just practice moving the exact minimum distance needed to avoid each punch.*

- *After you've done about 30 reps of that, get your hands into the proper punching position while slipping the next 30.*

- *Then, get your partner to vary their rhythm and be a little less predictable for the next 30 reps, so you have to watch their hands very carefully to see which hand is coming and when.*

- *Finally, practice another 30 reps where after every four or five punches slipped, you fire off a counter punch, not hitting your opponent, or just hitting a target mitt, and just practicing maintaining perfect punching form while slipping.*

Clinching Mistakes

Clinching is more of a last-resort defensive technique for when you're already stunned or hurt or just feeling overwhelmed by the opponent's offense. Therefore, get into the habit of practicing clinching near the end of a boxing session when you are exhausted, as that is when you are most prone to making mistakes. The most common errors to look out for are as follows:

- Loose grip - Not securing a tight enough grip around the opponent's body, head, or arms. This allows the opponent to easily break free or counterattack.

- Poor posture - Bending over too much or leaning too far forward during the clinch. This keeps you off balance,

- Leaving your vulnerable areas exposed such as the ribs, kidneys, or thighs.

- Not using footwork - Being stationary in the clinch allows your opponent to break free, reverse the position, or land effective counters.

- Not controlling the opponent's head, allowing them to strike, break away, or counter-clinch more easily.

7. Common Training Mistakes

As any great boxer will tell you, matches are won or lost in the gym, before you ever step into the ring. Barring freak injuries, illnesses, or other one-in-a-thousand events, the fighter that trains harder is almost always going to win the match. Therefore, now that we've covered and corrected common mentality and technical errors, it's time for a chapter on correcting common training and sparring mistakes to really ensure you're maximizing your training time and effort.

Training Too Fast

It's exciting to start a new training regime and launch yourself toward your goals of greatness. You imagine jumping right into the ring, going head-to-head in a boxing match, and having the referee hold up your gloved hand in victory, but pump the brakes!

As with anything worth doing, it will take time (lots of time). When we overtrain or start to implement too many changes all at once, we find ourselves tired, hungry, and depressed while simultaneously floundering at every turn, getting everything wrong, and falling on our faces... literally. Not only is training and fighting above your ability incredibly discouraging, but it is also dangerous—and not just for you. We can recognize when we've stumbled into this space when we think:

- *I'm too tired all of the time.*
- *This is just too hard.*
- *I hurt all over.*
- *I have noodle arms with no power.*
- *I'm too slow.*
- *My wife doesn't love me. (joking...)*

- *I'm tripping all over myself.*

- *I'm working so hard and not seeing any results.*

- *I was stronger/faster/better last week!*

These thoughts should be a red flag that you are training too hard or above your current ability. Listen to your trainer and your body; be patient, you'll get there. Everyone starts at the beginning. It's important to take rest days; this is true in any sport and boxing is no different. Finding balance in your training, diet, routine, and rest will actually allow your progression to be steady, even if you can't immediately see it. Boxing is a sport that should elevate your mood and mind, not drag you down so allow it to naturally guide your journey, giving each element—including yourself—its time and attention.

Remember that everybody is different, you may see your peers training twice a day making great progress to their goals and you may see people train twice a week making even better progress. There is no exact formula to this, just start slow and ramp it up as you train, you will eventually find that sweet spot.

Breaking Line of Sight

What's a normal reaction to throwing a punch? Closing your eyes! Well, if your eyes are closed, you will not only miss your target, but you won't see the attack coming right back at you. Closing your eyes is not the only mistake, blinking or flinching will be enough to throw you off your game and give your opponent a big advantage. Beginner boxers can struggle with keeping their line of sight because it's a natural response to divert or close your eyes instinctually and lose your focus. To correct this mistake, you can:

- *Practice maintaining eye contact with a sparring partner.*

- *Make sure to practice during offensive, defensive, and counter moves.*

- *Practice with a partner in slow motion to get a feel and understanding of the mechanics of different punches.*

- *Hold focus mitts for a partner to get comfortable with quick and aggressive movements toward your face.*

- *Use the double-end bag to train focus, rhythm, and to become accustomed to erratic movement.*

- *Continually train your footwork and defense—if you know you're quick and nimble in your movements, you'll have more confidence and avoid punches to the face.*

Wasting Energy

There are so many ways to waste energy in the ring and we've touched on quite a few:

- Stance:
    - *Too wide.*
    - *Knees too bent.*
    - *Leaning in the wrong direction.*
    - *Losing your stance.*
    - *Hanging your arms out from your body.*
- Getting tied up.
- Being too tight and tense.
- Becoming sloppy in your movements.
- Excessive footwork.
- Not wearing boxing shoes.
- Improper technique.
- Ineffectively cutting off the ring.

- Staying tense with your arms up and ready even when out of range.

- Moving too much while slipping and rolling.

- Beginning a match at full throttle and running out of steam.

Most, if not all, of these boil down to technique and training. So, to correct the tendency to waste energy, it's important to get to know your body and how it expends energy doing different things. You should focus on how to go about pacing for a match, taking into consideration that different boxers will set a different pace. Learning how to control the pace of a fight is to your benefit by training at a low and high intensity to switch up the pace and keep your opponent in a constant state of trying to catch up.

Too Much Focus on the Upper Body

There is a lot of truth to the phrase: "Don't skip leg day." Strong muscles are important for powerful punches; however, we don't just punch with our arms. In boxing, the entire body—including the hips, legs, knees, and core—is behind the force of our movement and a common mistake is to treat the upper body and lower body as two different components. The legs require much more attention than just focusing on footwork. Our lower body provides us with the means of balance, stability, and power. Even small movements of the lower body are important for generating maximum force.

Another mistake is to only be utilizing one leg at a time by transferring your weight between legs as you throw a punch. You should think of it more like a push-pull dynamic where each leg has an equal and opposite job to do to provide power, speed, and balance. Record yourself training shadow boxing drills or sparring and slow down the replay to really observe the utilization of your legs and where you are holding the weight with each movement. As you become more aware of how you're shifting your weight, you can practice pushing and pulling in a way that feels balanced between your legs.

Rule 1 and Rule 2 of Every Good Gym

These rules are so important and assumed that they are commonly taken for granted, but we'll put them down anyway because these are the rules that, if broken, are going to make your training time not just unproductive, but even dangerous. In fact, I'd go so far as to say that if a gym does not appear to be adhering to these rules, that's a major red flag, and personally, I'd go elsewhere.

Rule 1: Safety First

Many sports are dangerous and can cause injuries if people aren't careful, or even if they are, but combat sports are particularly so because the whole point, in a certain sense, is to cause injury of a certain kind to your opponent in order to win the match.

This can easily lead to a very dangerous and counterproductive mentality in training, however. As much as your goal in a boxing match is to win by landing better, cleaner, harder punches on your opponent in order to score a knockout or win on the judges' scorecards, your goal in training is absolutely not to 'win' training by scoring better, harder, cleaner punches on your training and sparring partners. On the contrary, your goal is to prepare yourself to win a match without getting hurt or hurting anyone else.

- *Therefore, when you're training and especially when you're sparring, remember that you're always trying to simulate the conditions of a real match without the actual dangerous parts of it, and the most dangerous part of boxing: punches to the head.*

- *When you're sparring or training, you should never be giving or taking hard punches to the head, even with headgear and oversized padded gloves.*

- *You should avoid, as much as possible, giving or taking any kind of light punches to the head.*

- *The reason is that as we have discovered over the last few decades, it's not just major blows that instantly cause concussions that cause brain damage over time.*

- *Even seemingly harmless 'knocks' to the head, when done thousands of times over the course of years, add up to a kind of brain damage called Chronic Traumatic Encephalopathy (CTE).*

For this reason, the first training mistake to avoid is anything that's going to be repeatedly impacting your head, even if you're wearing headgear and a mouthguard:

- *In order to practice your defense, work with a trusted training partner who will throw very light shots in a way that you can always defend or avoid them while doing proper techniques.*

- *The job of the training partner is to help you work on your defensive techniques and provide useful, instant feedback when you've made a mistake, not punish you by ringing your bell.*

- *Using other tools like foam nerf balls, foam pads, or even pool noodles to practice head movement and parrying and so on are also safer alternatives to actually having a guy throwing punches, even lightly, at your head.*

To work on your footwork and overall defense and offense with a partner in a realistic scenario without taking shots to the head:

- *Practice sparring without head punches allowed—body and shoulder punches only.*

- *To work on punching to the opponent's head with real power and bad intentions, do it with mitt work, a heavy bag, and a boxing dummy.*

- *Sparring with all punches allowed, like a real match, should only be done when preparing for a real amateur or professional bout, only a few times a week at most, and with a trusted partner that is not going to throw real power shots at your head and try to win a sparring match.*

- *Rather, your partner should help you work on your defensive game with light shots that give a realistic sense of a real match while doing the absolute minimum amount of real damage. Since the discovery and improved understanding of CTE, the days of "gym wars" are over.*

If you're asking yourself how to develop 'toughness' or your 'chin,' the answer is actually completely different from 'practicing' getting beat up. The answer to improving your toughness is actually:

- *Very intense cardio or high-intensity interval training (HIIT).*

- *Apart from a really solid punch to the liver (or groin, if you're male) or possibly breaking a bone in your hand, there's nothing that can happen to you in a boxing match that will physically hurt more than simple exhaustion.*

- *Making yourself extremely tired while training and learning how to push through that pain will make you tougher than getting hit.*

- *Punches stun you, knock you off balance, and may even knock you out, but none of that actually hurts more than the lactic acid flooding your muscles while every breath burns like fire in your lungs.*

- *To the extent that punches do hurt, they hurt way more when you're already tired.*

- *In order to be tough in the ring, be well-conditioned.*

- *In order to have 'heart' in the ring, be tireless.*

- *In order to have courage in the ring, be confident that you've trained harder than your opponent, that they will get tired before you, and that the longer the fight goes, the more your conditioning advantage will be apparent.*

- *Getting beat up in training doesn't help with any of that; it's beating yourself up with intense cardio workouts until you want to throw up, then pushing through anyway, that will really make you tough in the ring.*

Rule 2: No Ego

Ego is the biggest reason that people make mistakes in training. The biggest problem with ego is when it causes you to break Rule 1 and start going harder to try to 'win' training. That's not just dangerous, it's also counterproductive and just plain off-putting. Nobody wants to train with a person like that, and you'll quickly find yourself without any training partners if you're always trying to 'beat' them at training. Training is a cooperative endeavor where everyone is trying to make everyone else better together, not a zero-sum game where one fighter's 'wins' in training are others' 'losses.' By the same token, you should avoid training with anyone who seems like they're trying to 'win' training. Of course, there is nothing wrong with a bit of friendly competition in boxing, in fact it comes with many benefits, just try to tone it down a bit if you or anybody else takes it too far.

The second problem with ego is that it makes you way harder for a good coach or training to work with. If you don't trust your coach or trainer's advice, you shouldn't even be there at all; you should have chosen another coach or trainer you do trust in the first place. Arguing with them or ignoring them or whatever passive-aggressive resistance you might be contemplating is a huge waste of everyone's time, especially your own. That doesn't mean that you should just give blind trust to anyone and everyone; at a certain point, you do need to have some ego to stand up for yourself, believe in yourself, and put yourself on the line every day. It means that you need to make a decision to trust your coach, trainers, training partners, and then set your ego aside and devote yourself to simply absorbing everything you can and improving as much as you can while training.

If you're worried that your coach or some training partner is the one that has an ego and is using you to assuage their ego by bullying you in some way, which is a real thing that can happen, then what you need to do is find another gym or at least avoid that one nasty training partner. It's not your job to 'correct' their ego; your only job is to get better at boxing and the only opponent you need to beat every day is your own past self, by getting better.

Tips to Make Your Training More Effective

With Rule 1 and Rule 2 of training firmly in mind, here are some more specific tips to help you get the most out of every training session. There is so much to consider with boxing ranging from physical conditioning, technical skill, and mental sharpness, therefore it is a good idea that with each training session you have many points to reflect on instead of just being able to say you managed to punch the bag more times than last week.

Adhere to the Proper Training Cycle

The training cycle is how athletes learn and incorporate new techniques. A good coach already builds this into their sessions, but if you're training somewhat on your own or you're in a large gym where the coach cannot always be available to give you the kind of individual training you need at all times, you have to be your own coach sometimes, and that means you need to know and follow the training cycle yourself.

- The first part of the training cycle is choosing a specific technique you're going to work on.

- It could be your stance, your footwork, a specific punch or punch combination, a defensive technique, whatever.

- Once you've chosen it, watch yourself in the mirror doing the technique at normal speed, and see what flaws you can identify.

- Then, break the movement down into its most basic parts, and do the technique very slowly and carefully, trying to get it technically perfect in slow motion.

- Gradually speed up from there until you can repeat the technique perfectly at normal speed.

- Then repeat it at least 30 times.

- Depending on what the technique is, there will be other drills you can do related to the technique as well to keep the training more interesting and help you incorporate it into your broader game.

- Repetition is key here; remember what Bruce Lee said: "Do not fear the man who has practiced 10,000 kicks; fear the man who has practiced one kick 10,000 times."

Finally, make a conscious effort to incorporate this new technique into more realistic training scenarios like sparring or going rounds with a heavy bag. At first, it might feel like you're going backward because using a new unfamiliar technique or forcing yourself to use a technique you know you need to work on, will make you feel more awkward and less effective in a real sparring session, but these temporary 'setbacks' are a normal part of training and necessary to overcome in order to improve your skills overall. That's the training cycle for adding new techniques or improving old ones.

Proper Training Begins in Your Mind

There's a physical limit to how much your body can take for every day and week of training, but the mind does not have the same limitations. The real key to maximizing your training time is to focus your mind at all times on where you need to improve, how to improve, and what improvement will look like:

- *Always pay attention to each part of your body when learning or working on specific techniques.*

- *Always imagine how the technique will work in a real match.*

- *Always imagine there's an opponent in front of you, and how your technique will help you defeat them.*

- *Whether you're working on shadow boxing, a heavy bag, a partner holding mitts, whatever it may be, keep your mind sharp and focused on what you're doing and what an imaginary opponent may be doing.*

- *You can do this even while not physically training as well.*

- *And, importantly, you can do this while watching others train.*

- *You don't only have to learn from your own mistakes; the wisest learn from the mistakes of others.*

- *Whenever you see another boxer or training partner make a mistake, think about whether it's one you're making, too.*

- *Whatever advice you see given to that boxer, or whatever advice you think you might like to give them, give it to yourself, too.*

Working the Heavy Bag Properly

One thing that always stands out like a sore thumb in a boxing gym is a new boxer working the heavy bag improperly because it always starts swinging around wildly after they throw just a few punches and then they have to catch it, reset it, and start over again without ever really building up a nice rhythm. One of the side benefits of working with a heavy bag is building up your timing and rhythm in order to avoid this problem.

- *The key to preventing the bag from swinging around wildly is to time your combinations so that you're hitting the bag just as soon as it starts swinging back toward you, which usually means you have to take a small step forward after throwing your first punches.*

- *You want to catch the bag at the end of its swing and keep it there to keep it from swinging back or around wildly.*

- *If you let it swing back towards you before you start your punch, you'll stop it dead for sure, but you'll also hurt your wrist with the impact.*

- *If you let it swing all the way back and then punch it, you'll just make it swing way faster on the next go around.*

The second key to working the heavy bag once you've learned the timing to keep it from going crazy is to practice realistically, like it's a real match.

- *That means keeping your hands up, moving your head, and practicing your footwork. Step around the heavy bag and change up angles.*

- *Move inside and work it in close, practice a clinch or practice avoiding getting clinched, then step back and work it outside as well.*

- *Finally, and perhaps most importantly, set up a timer and give yourself 2 or 3-minute rounds with 1-minute rest periods in between.*

Get a feel for how to pace yourself in a real match. If you throw non-stop at full power, you'll wear yourself out in seconds. Practice:

- *Setting up your range and combos with quick jabs.*

- *Feints.*

- *Hard but not full-power punches.*

- *Quick combinations that end with one good power shot, not everything thrown at a hundred percent.*

- *Breathing out on every punch.*

- *Keeping your eyes on the opponent at all times.*

- *Avoiding imaginary punches coming in and throwing perfect counters.*

8. Continuous Improvement

This book was written to help you learn from your own mistakes and show you that mistakes are nothing to fear or get frustrated by; they're just a healthy and productive part of the process. This book was also written to help you learn from my mistakes, too. Every possible mistake I've written about is something that I did when I was first learning to box, and every solution I've described was what worked for me. The hardest part of correcting mistakes is understanding where exactly the mistake is coming from:

- *So many punching mistakes come from a poor stance.*

- *So many defensive mistakes come from bad training habits of just losing vision and awareness of the opponent.*

- *So many matches are lost because of an inexperienced boxer fighting with every muscle tensed and holding their breath in every combination causing them to run out of energy in the second round.*

All these mistakes come from bad habits in training going unnoticed until they become catastrophically apparent. A great coach can help you find and break these bad habits as soon as possible, but not everyone has the benefit of a great coach's undivided attention at all times. That's where this book, and you, come in. You can be your own great coach, you can learn to find and correct your own mistakes, and you can learn to love the process of doing so. Boxing is hard, but there's nothing more rewarding than overcoming your own physical and mental hurdles to better yourself, and then proving it, in and out of the ring.

It's generally much easier to see another boxer's mistakes than your own. Even if you're looking in the mirror, what you're doing may feel 'right' to you even if it isn't. Although I've told you many times to focus your attention, there are so many things to pay attention to, from your own body to your position relative to your opponent, to your opponent's body, to your breathing, to your plans and trying to anticipate your opponent, it's just impossible to focus on everything at once and very hard to know what to focus on most at any given second.

However, when you're watching another boxer, you can focus all your attention on them and none on yourself, and that can help you see their mistakes more easily. Once you can do that, then you can learn to turn that kind of attention on yourself and see if you aren't making the same kinds of mistakes and would benefit from the same kinds of advice. It was learning to do that really helped me take my own game to the next level, and I believe anyone else could do the same thing. Finally, below are some tips to aid you with continuous improvement.

- Constantly work on remaining calm and composed under pressure. Mental resilience is key to handling tough situations in a fight. Make an attempt to include meditation, deep breathing exercises, and mindfulness in your routine.

- Use visualization techniques before training and fights to mentally rehearse movements, scenarios, and combinations. Picture yourself succeeding in various situations, such as countering punches or landing key combinations.

- Enter every sparring session or fight with a strategy in mind. Analyze your opponent's strengths and weaknesses and devise a plan to exploit them. Adapt your game plan as needed throughout the fight.

- Recognize that boxing is a long-term journey. Focus on small, consistent improvements rather than expecting rapid success. Trust the process and aim for steady growth.

- Be open to criticism and feedback from coaches, sparring partners, or even yourself after watching footage. Use constructive feedback to guide your training and work on areas needing improvement.

- Focus on a well-balanced diet with sufficient protein, carbs, and healthy fats to fuel training and recovery. Stay hydrated and ensure you're eating nutrient-dense foods that support your energy needs.

- Aim for 7-9 hours of sleep per night. Quality sleep is crucial for muscle recovery, mental clarity, and maintaining peak performance levels during training.

- Include active recovery days in your routine with light jogging, yoga, or stretching. This helps your body recuperate while maintaining flexibility and mobility.

- Avoid overtraining by recognizing the signs of fatigue, injury, or burnout. Rest when necessary to prevent injuries and allow for optimal recovery.

- Sparring is where you apply everything you've learned in real-time against an opponent. Spar regularly but intelligently—don't over-spar and risk injury, but use it as an opportunity to refine skills, test strategies, and gain experience.

- Challenge yourself by sparring with a variety of partners who have different styles, sizes, and skill levels. This will help you adapt to different situations and improve your versatility.

- Dedicate some sparring sessions solely to defense. Work on blocking, slipping, and footwork while limiting your offensive output. This helps develop strong defensive habits.

- Train under pressure to simulate the stress of a real fight. Perform drills while fatigued, practice in chaotic settings, and engage in high-intensity sparring rounds to build your mental fortitude.

- Stay disciplined with your training schedule. Consistency is the key to improvement, whether it's training technique, fitness, or sparring.

- Continuously set short-term and long-term goals to stay motivated and track your progress. These can include improving specific techniques, mastering combinations, or conditioning targets.

- Stay humble and never stop learning. Boxing is a lifelong process, and there is always something new to improve. Keep an open mind, and approach every session with the mentality of learning something new.

Conclusion

In this book, we covered your entire boxing game and how to find mistakes and correct them. We began with the most important foundation for tackling any difficult, complex task: your mindset and your mental preparation and organization. Before you accomplish any major goal, you need to understand the goal completely and how to get there, step by step. You need to be positive and have rational optimism, you need to be open to finding and correcting mistakes, and you need to be expecting setbacks and be mentally ready to overcome them one by one until you accomplish the goal.

After going over your mental game, we started with the most basic technical aspect of boxing, your stance, and progressed logically from there, with footwork, punching and offense, and defensive techniques. We covered the most common errors at each step, and specific advice and drills for how to avoid those errors or correct them as efficiently as possible. Then, we talked about training and learning from mistakes in general.

If there's one thing you take away from this book, I hope it's that you go from fearing or being frustrated by errors to learning to value the process of discovering your own mistakes and learning to correct and overcome them. Now that you've gotten all the tools and advice from an experienced trainer who struggled for years, I know you'll get on with accomplishing your dreams for boxing faster and even more enjoyably than I did. Remember, the only way to stop sucking at boxing is to put the work in, so what are you waiting for?

References

Be Happy Boxing. (2020, January 15). *8 common beginner mistakes in boxing*. Be Happy Boxing. https://behappyboxing.com/8-common-beginner-mistakes-in-boxing/

BoxRec. (2017). *BoxRec: Floyd Mayweather Jr*. Boxrec.com. https://boxrec.com/en/proboxer/352

Coach Aaron. (2018, January 13). *Get lean, build muscle, learn to box-for fitness or competition*. Commando Boxing. https://commandoboxing.com/10-technique-errors-all-boxers-should-watch-out-for

Concussion Legacy Foundation. (2018, November 6). *What is CTE?* Concussion Legacy Foundation. https://concussionfoundation.org/CTE-resources/what-is-CTE

Csikszentmihalyi, M. (1975). *Beyond boredom and anxiety*. Jossey-Bass Publishers.

Dynamic Striking. (2021). *Stance switching drill with Stephen "Wonderboy" Thompson*. dynamicstriking.com. https://dynamicstriking.com/blogs/news/stance-switching-drill-with-stephen-wonderboy-thompson

Easter, M. (2021, June 4). *Use the '20-5-3' rule to make yourself happier and stronger.* Men's Health. https://www.menshealth.com/fitness/a36547849/how-much-time-should-i-spend-outside/?utm_source=pocket-newtab

Gloveworx. (2021). *5 jump rope techniques that will make you a better boxer.* gloveworx.com. https://www.gloveworx.com/blog/5-jump-rope-techniques-will-make-you-better-boxer/

Ho, L. (2017, July 31). *Straight to Boxing.* Straight to Boxing. https://straight2boxing.com/

IMDB. (n.d.). *Million Dollar Baby (2004).* Www.imdb.com. https://www.imdb.com/title/tt0405159/characters/nm0000151

Imrus. (2021, July 19). *6 basic boxing punches & how to throw them correctly.* Punchingbagsguide.com. https://punchingbagsguide.com/basic-boxing-punches-guide/

InFighting. (2019). *The 77 most common mistakes in boxing.* www.infighting.com. https://www.infighting.ca/kickboxing/the-77-most-common-mistakes-in-boxing/#BOXING_MISTAKE_2-_Pumping_the_Jab

Jeffries, T. (n.d.). *Master boxer*. Www.masterboxing.com. https://www.masterboxing.com/

Juma, A. (2016, February 19). *Socrates on the secret to success*. Aly Juma. https://alyjuma.com/success/

Karageorghis, C. I., & Terry, P. C. (2011). *Inside sport psychology*. Human Kinetics.

Knight, A. (2020, April 20). Boxing footwork: A complete guide. healthyprincipals.com. https://www.healthyprinciples.co.uk/boxing-footwork/

Miller, C. A., Frisch, M. B., & Latham, G. P. (2020). *Creating your best life: The ultimate life list guide*. Sterling Publishing Co.

MyBoxingCoach.com. (2010, January 26). *The boxing stance–do it right!* Www.myboxingcoach.com. https://www.myboxingcoach.com/stance-and-on-guard/

Nguyen, J. (2011, July 26). *The perfect training pace*. ExpertBoxing. https://expertboxing.com/the-perfect-training-pace

Nguyen, J. (2012, October 9). *10 boxing footwork tips*. ExpertBoxing. https://expertboxing.com/10-boxing-footwork-tips

Nguyen, J. (2013, January 7). *Boxing jump rope training guide*. ExpertBoxing. https://expertboxing.com/boxing-jump-rope-training-guide

Nguyen, J. (2020, December 18). *Secrets to boxing defense*. ExpertBoxing. https://expertboxing.com/secrets-to-boxing-defense

Nguyen, J. (2021, May 26). *Power punching secrets, part 1*. ExpertBoxing. https://expertboxing.com/power-punching-secrets-part-1-2-legged-punching

Peterson, J. B. (2021). *Beyond order: 12 more rules for life*. Random House Of Canada.

Pullman, J. (2020, October 1). *Pullmans Gym* [Video]. YouTube. https://www.youtube.com/channel/UCnWhDyhWyOzplLXo5oBHMpg

Richardson, T., & Gilman, R. T. (2019). Left-handedness is associated with greater fighting success in humans. *Scientific Reports*, 9(1). https://doi.org/10.1038/s41598-019-51975-3

Sands, F. (2014, December 16). *Advanced boxing footwork: The stance switch*. myboxingcoach.com. https://www.myboxingcoach.com/advanced-boxing-footwork-stance-switch/

Tate, J. (2011, January 24). *The 50 greatest boxing quotes of all time*. Bleacher Report. https://bleacherreport.com/articles/575189-50-greatest-boxing-quotes-of-all-time

Van Veldhuysen, J. (n.d.). *Precision striking blog*. The Ultimate Boxing Experience. https://precisionstriking.com/blog/

Yormark, N. (2020, January 15). *10 ways to transform negative thoughts to achieve your goals*. Inspiyr.com. https://inspiyr.com/10-ways-to-transform-negative-thoughts-to-achieve-your-goals/